# Primary Columns

## The 2012 GOP Presidential Campaign

Also by Patrick W. Griffin:

*Pay No Attention To That Man Behind the Curtain:*
*How Technology Has Made Traditional Advertising Obsolete*

# PRIMARY COLUMNS

## The 2012 GOP Presidential Campaign

*In Essays, Op-Eds, Blog Posts, Musings, and Rants!*

Patrick W. Griffin

Foreword by Alex Castellanos

BLUEFIELD PUBLISHING

First published in August 2012 by Bluefield Publishing, an imprint of StyleMatters Writing Services, LLC.

ISBN: 978-1-938954-01-6
Printed in the United States of America
First Edition

**Library of Congress Cataloguing-in-Publication Data**

Griffin, Patrick W.
    Primary columns: the 2012 GOP presidential campaign in essays, op-eds, blog posts, musings and rants / Patrick W. Griffin
        p. cm.
    ISBN: 978-1-938954-01-6 (pbk.)
    1. Humor.   2. Political Science.   I. Title
    Library of Congress Control Number: 2012914134

**To Dad,** the funniest, smartest guy I ever knew. I miss your smile, your wisdom, and most of all your unconditional love.

# CONTENTS

# AUTHOR'S NOTE

**This book uses the words** and actions of others to illustrate points which are factual as I know them to have occurred. Where the dialogue attributed to an actual individual appears within quotation marks, it comes from that speaker, writer, or publication and is used "as reposted." Where the dialogue is not in quotation marks, or is otherwise indirectly quoted, it has been paraphrased, reflecting only a lack of certainty about the precise wording used by the individual and not the nature, intention, or tone of the statement. In addition, Chapters presented in the form of a "Memorandum" are completely fictitious in nature and do not represent actual communication between the parties.

# FOREWORD

## *by Alex Castellanos*

**Who would have thought** that the 2012 election would have been the strangest, wildest, most unpredictable gladiatorial contest ever?

Newt Gingrich, a man named after a small, brightly colored salamander, runs for President. What could possibly go wrong? It turns out that Newt, the candidate, not the weak-limbed amphibian, was very good with ideas but not good with another thing you find often in politics: people. Gingrich left the campaign trail millions of dollars in debt -- and that was just to Tiffany's.

There was Rick Perry, who led the race until he made the tragic mistake of actually running for President. Perry proved the old adage that some things are better seen and not heard. Apparently, no one had told Perry we would be required to answer questions! Rick Perry was a lot like a coffee-table book: a lot of pretty pictures but not much text there.

Herman Cain, the happiest warrior in the field, nearly captured the Republican nomination just by repeating his area code. The former Godfather's Pizza CEO advocated the "9-9-9 Plan" to restore the economy. Cain, who proudly declared he could not name the President of Ubeki-beki-beki-stan-stan, proved that it may occasionally be a good idea to use a tele-tele-prompter-prompter.

And who would have thought that the most conservative, bible-backing candidate in the GOP field would have become a fashion-trendsetter, making the sweater vest a dress-for-success essential? Rick Santorum left Republicans warmer than he found them, a more significant contribution than many other candidates can claim.

At some point in the roller-coaster ride, nearly all GOP candidates climbed to the top, establishing themselves as frontrunners, only to plunge to the bottom. This included the Sarah Palin of 2012, Michelle Bachman. The mother of 23 foster kids, all teenage girls, Bachman had so many children, she didn't know what to do. At least she didn't live in a shoe.

And let us remember Ron Paul, who didn't win a single primary, unless you count those on his home planet. And who can forget Tim Pawlenty? As it turns out, almost everyone.

In the end, the only Republican left standing was Mitt Romney. Romney surprised the field with inspired discipline or unimaginative determination, depending on your point of view. Romney ground his way through what seemed like 150 GOP primaries and caucuses, quite a remarkable accomplishment since we have only 50 states.

And debates! 2012 was the year we found out it was legal to have more debates than candidates! Even Romney himself was nearly disqualified from the race after Newt beat him in South Carolina when it was revealed that Romney was unfairly good looking.

Remarkable times produce remarkable campaigns. This 2012 primary season finds the United States at an unusually perilous and promising moment.

In this election, a contest like we've never seen, the United States stands on the edge of a precipice. We are choosing whether to fall or fly. We are determining whether the greatest country in the world will plunge over the edge into the abyss or to soar to heights we've never known.

Historically, the United States has always considered itself ascendant. We have always thought tomorrow would be better than today, that our children would have better opportunities than we have known. This has always been the country of endless promise and limitless frontiers. But not today.

Today, we doubt. We think we may no longer be climbing skyward, but rather tumbling over the hump, staring down at our own decline. We fear what is next. For the first time in history, a majority of Americans report that they no longer think their children will have more and better opportunities than they have enjoyed.

We crave renewal. As Peggy Noonan writes, our country believes "we have one more comeback left in us." We are looking for leaders like Moses to take us to the Promised Land.

It is this moment that the big heart and entertaining mind of Pat Griffin documents in the essays, op-eds, blog posts and rants collected here—with grace, insight and have-to-laugh humor.

Most people don't know that Pat Griffin, long ago, invented politics in New Hampshire, shortly after man discovered fire, the wheel, and the effect of whacking your opponent with a club. Pat was one of the first media-consultants to bring modern combative marketing practices from the world of advertising to politics.

He did this in New Hampshire, no less, where elections are the official state industry. Not everyone can play with the big boys in New Hampshire. The Granite State is *the* political theme park, the Disneyland of politics. Here, Pat not only blazed the trail but also achieved great success, electing a swath of political leaders some as disreputable, conniving and self-serving as the wonderful American people they represent. No one has more fun poking fun at the process he knows so well. I first met Pat over two decades ago in the wild New Hampshire political jungles. He served as my guide, Sherpa, counselor and good friend. Talking politics with Pat Griffin is never an exercise in cynicism. This is a man who loves his country; its people and its promise. The tongue is sharp, the mind is hopeful, and the heart is pure.

Perhaps you've wondered if President Obama is really as competent as we are told, since our economy is melting down, half the world is on fire and our money is turning to toilet paper. If so, you will want to read "The Don Knotts Presidency" and how "this President, like Barney Fife, is patently unprepared and unable to do his job." Next time you watch the news, you'll no doubt think about the Deputy from Mayberry and the "Fifeing" of America. After you join Pat behind enemy lines as he goes undercover to "Occupy Wall Street," with his dogs Rocky and Fenway to protect him, you may never go to a Chinese restaurant again!

Pat Griffin is one of the brightest guys in politics and one of the funniest people on earth. If you are not fortunate enough to spend a day in his company, read this book and laugh out loud as immovable political objects meet an irresistible force: the delicious mind of Pat Griffin.

**Alex Castellanos**
Friday, July 13, 2012

# ACKNOWLEDGMENTS

**Let me begin by** thanking my friend Alex Castellanos for agreeing to provide a thoughtful and witty introduction to this book. Alex and I share a love for politics, boating, and cigars as well as a mutual love for the practice of campaign media going back to the 1992 re-election campaign of President George H.W. Bush, where we first met "in the trenches." Alex is a smart and insightful practitioner of the trade. He has a great talent for the written word, spot-on instincts, and a perfect sense of strategic timing for what to say and do when. All that and yet he still agreed to help me with this project. Perhaps his judgment is waning.

I also want to thank my colleague at GY&K Nathaniel Grimes. Nate has worked by my side on both corporate and political clients for nearly 3 years. He is smart, savvy, and mature beyond his years. Nate's oversight, editorial control, and a true gift for spelling and grammar have made my writing only marginally better. It is his sense of organization, communication skill, creativity, and patience that have been most helpful in allowing me to meet deadlines and avoid being car bombed, (at least up until now). In addition to this book, Nate was also critical to the success of my first book, *Pay No Attention to That Man Behind the Curtain*. Thanks, Nate, for your collaborative and productive nature and for covering my ass for so many years.

I also want to thank Neil Levesque, the Director of The New Hampshire Institute of Politics at Saint Anselm College in Manchester, New Hampshire. Neil suggested that I might enjoy doing a fellowship at the Institute during the 2011-12 Academic year in the heart of a presidential primary year. I must say it was one of the best experiences of my life and I have developed an enormous respect for both the NHIOP and the amazing talent of its faculty, staff and the students I have had the privilege to work with over the course of my one year in academia. When the political world descends on New Hampshire, the Institute is the center of the universe. The NHIOP played an important role in allowing me both the time, state of mind, and access to the 2012 GOP Primary campaign which helped contribute to this tome. To Meghan Gill, a Saint Anselm student who has helped coordinate the details of this book and who is a shining example of the quality of student the NHIOP attracts and perpetuates, a thank you for helping the written word get to the printed page precisely. As an intern at our firm, Meghan jumped into this project and essentially this one young woman did the work of ten men. I'm fairly certain that Meghan will either serve as the first female President of the United States or as Chairman of the Federal Reserve. Either way our nation would be the better for it!

Thanks to Bluefield Publishing for their patience and assistance, to my assistant Tina Yanuszewski and to all of my colleagues at Griffin York & Krause for allowing me the time over the last year and half to cobble this book together.

And to all who toil in the noble profession of politics from the candidates to the consultants, from the media who cover the campaigns to the guys who bang signs into snowbanks, from the phone bankers to the door knockers, and most especially to the voters in early primary and caucus states. None of what you read here would have been possible without you. Neither would the strength of our Republic. Long live the nominating process of early caucus and primary states!

"It's been said that politics is the second oldest profession. I have learned that it bears a striking resemblance to the first."

— **Ronald Reagan**

Photo by Gage Skidmore

**Mitt Romney:**
as the Front-Runner

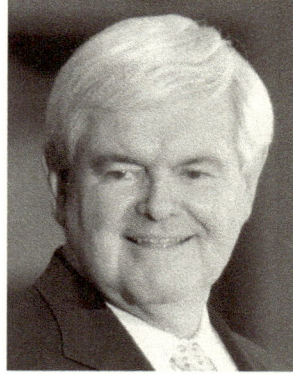

Photo by Gage Skidmore

**Rick Santorum:**
as the Authentic
Conservative

Congressional photo

**Ron Paul:**
as the Supreme Commander
of the Red Planet

# THE PLAYERS

Photo by Gage Skidmore

**Newt Gingrich:**
as the Professor

Photo by Gage Skidmore

**Herman Cain:**
as the Candidate Not Ready
For Prime Time

**Rick Perry:**
as the Governor
of Texas

Photo by Gage Skidmore

**Jon Huntsman:**
as the Resume
Candidate

Official State Photo

**Chris Christie:**
as the Un-Candidate

Photo by David Shankbone

**George W. Bush:**
as the Great Comunicatorist

White House photo by Eric Draper

**Sarah Palin:**
as Herself

Photo by Gage Skidmore

# INTRODUCTION

**It was January eighth, 2012,** and I found myself at a small Mexican/Caribbean restaurant on the east side of Manchester, New Hampshire. On this cold Sunday afternoon, just two days before the New Hampshire presidential primary, I had made my way to this little known ethnic eatery tucked in a seedy strip mall next to an even seedier bowling alley, in order to witness for myself a rally and "Meet and Greet" with former House Speaker, and would-be GOP presidential nominee, Newt Gingrich.

My old pal Mike Murphy was visiting from the west coast and we were in the quadrennial epi-center of American politics for the "First in the Nation" Presidential Primary. It was the first time in many years that neither Mike nor I were working for a presidential campaign and while it felt a little odd, we both agreed it was way more fun this way: traveling the state at our own pace, stopping at various candidate events and rallies, and just plain observing the strange goings-on that made the New Hampshire Kabuki Dance so fascinating.

We found a parking place not far from the massive Gingrich campaign bus, assuring us we had found in fact found the correct—albeit unlikely—venue for the Gingrich event. As we made our way around the building and toward the front entrance, we were intercepted by a collection of the kind of malcontents one only sees days before the Iowa caucus or the presidential primary in New Hampshire: the overly caffeinated and highly passionate professional protesters—*en masse*! Murphy and I agreed that of all our stops on this particular day the "nut factor," as we liked to call it, was exceptionally high here for Newt. The Occupy Wall Street loons were there banging drums and playing kazoos, while chanting something about Mitt Romney and the one percent. There were the pro-life folks with graphic, often offensive posters of mutilated humanity; the pro-choice crowd cackling about politicians keeping their hands off their collective bodies—even a group of Orthodox Jews protesting the occupation of the West Bank with giant banners stood silently along the perimeter. Protesting Orthodox Jews? This was a first!

There was the pro-hemp contingent, hoping presumably that with their presence, Newt might somehow miraculously endorse the sudden legalization of cannabis. Their group got best prop of the day by sporting what was left of a 1980s Toyota Corolla (thickly rusted, paint job near-gone, and its front bumper attached with what appeared to be a child's jump rope) topped by a gigantic pot ball tied to the roof! The pot ball was actually as big as the car itself. I politely suggested to one of their contingent that they might want to be at Ron Paul's event, which was being held on the other side of the state. Paul was on record as being far more sympathetic to their cause. Unfortunately, the guy was too stoned to know what I was talking about.

Inside, the venue was packed with Newt supporters: a lot of cops and private security types (presumably protecting Gingrich from the mob outside), tons of tired and grumpy national press types, and somewhere in the scrum, presumably Gingrich himself. I could hear him but not see him, as the restaurant itself was a dark rabbit warren of small windowless rooms packed well beyond what I presumed to be within the limits of the fire code. Sound was piped in over the restaurant's tinny Muzak sound system. Everyone looked exhausted. Gingrich staffers, the faithful, and especially the press looked like they had been on a month-long bender—in fact they had. Most of these poor souls had been on the road for months prior to the Iowa caucus the week before, sleeping in bad hotels, couch-surfing at the homes of friends and volunteers, eating drive-through fast food (when they had time to eat), and drinking stale coffee, Diet Coke, Red Bull, or all of the above—simply to remain conscious. Looking at them, I realized that not that long ago I had been one of them. Bone-tired, jet-lagged. Back and forth from Iowa to New Hampshire, and on and on and on. Presidential political campaigns are like *Groundhog Day*, the Bill

Murray movie where with each wakeup call you find that every day is exactly the same!

Murphy and I hung around for a bit, chatting with some friends we knew in the press corps. We shared stories of campaigns gone by and prognosticated the likely outcome of the primary and general elections, like baseball fans sitting around the proverbial hot stove in the dead of winter, futilely attempting to predict who would win that year's World Series.

There was, however, no real steam in the room; it was without energy. Newt began droning on about reforming America's immigration system—an interesting topic to tackle in a Mexican/Caribbean joint. When he mentioned the word "deportation" I could just picture the dishwashers and kitchen staff dashing for the back door and relative sanctuary of the alley.

We finally left the place. Thankfully, at least some of the demonstrators were still there, although outside I was sorry to see no sign of the dilapidated Toyota and the giant pot ball. I assumed those guys must have suddenly become inexplicably hungry and had likely gone looking for a thousand pizzas.

For the sake of our Republic, I remain hopeful that early primaries and caucus events such as this one remain a staple of our democratic elective process—especially as each campaign for the oval office seemingly becomes more important than the last, with the stakes growing higher every four years. Once again, we were all hearing the politicians on all sides saying the same familiar thing: "This election will be the most important in our lives!"

I begin by recounting this one stop—one of many I had the chance to observe during the 2012 GOP nomination process, from Iowa to New Hampshire and from South Carolina to Florida and beyond—because it is representative of the thousands of such "retail" events that candidates must produce (and endure) over the course of the presidential nomination process. It starts in living rooms and at kitchen tables, in places like Manchester and Keene, Des Moines and Waterloo, and in cities, towns, and precincts across the country in early primary and caucus states. The more you think about the marathon that seeking the presidency actually is, the more you have to wonder—what kind of person would ever really want the job? The answer: plenty.

In the 2012 GOP primary, there were a total of 27 nationally televised GOP presidential debates—which many, including me, believe did not serve the candidates, their campaigns, or the democratic process particularly well. Primaries and caucuses, especially the early ones, are meant to be one-on-one with the voters. The whole idea of Iowa, New Hampshire, and South Carolina is to allow candidates and voters the chance to actually connect, to size each other up, and as Daniel Webster once said, to "take measure of the man" (woman). Candidates crazy enough to actually run for President are forced to attend retail political events by the hundreds, if not thousands. They must be prepared to endure answering more questions about any given issue than one human should be expected; but endure they do, and that is what makes the process so pure and noble. These chapters are mere snapshots, as I saw them, of candidates and their campaigns on the way to the nomination. Primaries, debates, debacles, attack ads, campaign promises, and policy speeches come and go quickly during the compressed nominating process of modern campaigning. I have tried to pick through and include something about at least all of the major candidates of 2012, and a few minor ones as well. I am both humbled and amused by the way things I wrote and predicted one week would change in a matter of days, or even hours, in a digital campaign world with an endless news cycle. Sometimes I was right—sometimes not even close. I've had the chance to work on a lot of campaigns. I've won and lost; at the end of the day very few political hacks like me, no matter how much experience we may have, ever really get it all right. That's what makes it so fun.

The bizarre ritual of nominating and electing a President of the United States happens every three years or so. It begins in restaurants, church basements, town hall meetings, ice cream socials, and on endless bus tours. Not just in New Hampshire, but also in Iowa, Florida, South Carolina, Nevada, Michigan, Colorado, Wisconsin, and Illinois... and the list goes on. Nearly every state in the union has its turn to host the menagerie that is the presidential primary. The early states seem to matter more.

I wrote these columns in real time as the candidates, potential candidates, and would-be contenders began to line up, sign up, or drop out of the race for the 2012 GOP nomination. This nominating year was a bit less interesting than 2008. This year, with President Obama unchallenged in the Democratic primary, it was just we Republicans who ate each other's young. The pace and spectacle in each of the early primary and caucus states is slightly less frenetic when only one party is fully engaged in the process of elective politics, but it is frenetic nonetheless.

This tome is comprised of a series of blog posts, op-eds and columns I was able to write during the course of the year leading up to the 2012 nomination. I wrote them up through Super Tuesday, when it became clear that the field had finally, thankfully, winnowed. At last, we knew for certain who the GOP nominee would be—the man who'd amassed the required 1,144 GOP delegates to secure the nomination at the party's convention in Tampa, Florida.

I have arranged these columns and posts in the chronological order in which I wrote them and subsequently posted or published them. As I've said, like most political prognosticators I made predictions, gave advice, and editorialized about the state of the race, the issues of the day, what could or would happen, and how I thought things would turn out in the end. For the most part, the 2012 primary campaign held few surprises, other than the fact that it lumbered on as long as it did. But what's fun about this book is the freedom I felt in writing the things I did. Not working for a campaign or candidate or committee or Super PAC or special interest gives one immense freedom. In many ways I found that I was able to look at things more dispassionately and more openly (although still plenty partisan). It was, as they say, a thoroughly liberating experience. I can honestly say that the 2012 primary contest, beginning in Iowa and un-officially ending with the Texas primary on May 28, 2012, was the most fun I've ever had! During the campaign, I wrote, offered political commentary on network and cable television, and had the chance to serve as a Senior Fellow at the New Hampshire Institute of Politics at Saint Anselm College—a place where I learned far more from the students then I could ever have taught them.

Our democracy is not perfect, much like the old adage about sausage-making: it's not real pretty to watch. But at the end of the day, what more democratic way to pick the next possible leader of the free world than to subject him or her to a series of exhausting contests held state by state and town by town, where voters have the chance to take such intimate measure of each candidate?

I'm a great fan of the history of early primary and caucus campaigns: the twists and turns, the roller-coaster ride of gaffes, and the moments of rhetorical, strategic, and tactical brilliance. A presidential campaign, truth be told, is like three-dimensional chess on steroids. Every move elicits a counter-move and commensurate repercussions. It's all done on a high wire—no tether, no safety harness, no net. Running for President is the toughest job in America, and the best test of skill, temperament, ideas, courage and patriotism required of the person who ultimately is elected to do the job. It's easy to be cynical, to second-guess the candidates, campaigns, strategists and media who create all the hoopla. But at the end of the day, only in America can we truly respect and understand our extraordinary election process—for it is uniquely and unabashedly American and (almost always) results in the best candidate becoming President.

In these chapters I try, with tongue often firmly planted in cheek, to offer my opinions and insights on the bizarre nature of elective democracy we all experienced in 2012. I think I have done my job well, because I received an equal amount of threats and hate mail from all sides—and just about every campaign (the recently hired food tester has been well worth the investment as he doubles as a car-starter as well!)

It is my hope that you will find the columns, essays, op-eds, blog posts, musings, and rants contained herein both informative and interesting, and most of all that at the very least, here and there they make you smile.

**Patrick W. Griffin**
July 2012
Boston, Massachusetts

# DEAR SARAH:
## *What Would George W. Bush Say of Palin's Lexicon?*

Sarah Palin has taken time off the campaign trail just long enough to set the political establishment on fire after posting (are you ready for this?) a nonexistent word in a recent Tweet. The offending word was "refudiate," a combination of the verb "refute" and "repudiate." We all know pretty much what she meant, and she's certainly not the first politician to mangle the English language.

I have to wonder what my friend and former client, Ol' George W. Bush, might be thinking about all of this. After all, Bush was a President who made his share of "misprognostications," and who was "misunderestimated" (to use his word) by the effete elite Main Stream Media for years. What if the former President were to jot a note off to "Mama Grizzly" just to let her know that he feels her pain? I wonder what that note might look like...

*Dear Sarah,*

*Hope you and all your cubs are doing well up there on the Russian front!*

*Laura and I have immensively enjoyed our time relaxicating here at the ranch in Crawford. Laura has taken up crochetering, which allows her to make wonderful plant holders and wall hangerations that really warm up the ranch!*

*I, on the other hand, spend much of the day excercizering on my mountain bike, jogging and decamouflagering the property with my chain saw. It's real man's work, and it helps me to relaxify myself quite well.*

*I am also spending time putting the finishing touches on my autobiological book due out in the late fall just before electrification day. All said, we are well and enjoying retirementation to its fullest.*

*I've read about all this brouhaha generationed by your recent commentical words about trying to refudiate the failed policies of "Smarty Pants" and his advisorialists in the White House and Congress. I don't care what the* New York Times *says; I think you're right on the money! It's pretty clear Americans are fed up with this cat Obama and that they long for some common-sensification when it comes to jobs, the economy and our foreign polinization regarding the War on Terror.*

*Don't let their recriminationilism get you down!*

*I know exactly what you meant—more importantly, so do most American citerizationarians. Obama's liberal policies, high taxes, trillion-dollar budget defecations, and a jobless recovery are all things the voters will definitely choose to "refudiate" at the polls come November. Be sure to keep up the good work! Don't let Comrade Matthews and that former sports castration guy Keith Olbermann get you down. America needs articulitarianisim practiced by true patriots, and you, my friend, define that role!*

*Laura and I are proud of your good work and your reinventionism of words that appropriately articulify the American people's understandable frustrationism with the current administration's lack of leadership and bad policification.*

*Our very best wishes to Todd and your 36 children and grandchildren.*

*Warm and kind regards,*
*George W. Bush*


Say what you want about the words Bush might use or Palin, in fact did use. I get exactly what they're saying. Most Americans are so angry with Obama and the Democrats that they can't effectively put into words their sense of frustration and disappointment and anger. I suggest

Republicans start hand-painting signs that say REFUDIATE OBAMA AND PELOSI! Or there's the ever popular, REFUDIATE OBAMA-CARE! They'd be a big hit, and I predict that T-shirt and bumper stickers sales will be brisk.

If "refudiate" combines "repudiating" the current administration's policies and "refuting" the nonsensical politics of division foisted upon us by these clowns, I'm for it! Remember, way back when, there was a time when "Google" wasn't a word either!

★

# CHAPTER TWO

## TINA FEY MIGHT DISAGREE:
### *Five reasons Sarah Palin should not run for President*

Sarah Palin has been making noise again about jumping into the GOP race for the White House, but she needs to think about this decision carefully. The question she needs to be asking herself is not "Can I win?" She can't. The real question: should she ruin the trailer by actually making the movie?

There is nothing worse than a movie trailer that gives away the entire plot of the film, showing all the best scenes. Palin makes for a pretty good trailer, but she's no full-length feature, which is what Republicans need in a nominee to deny President Obama a second term. She has already played the main supporting role in a national campaign, and that didn't work out so well for the GOP. Palin is a much better "possible candidate" than actual candidate. By announcing that she is a candidate for President, Sarah Palin loses the one potent thing that makes her relevant: the possibility that she might run. It's titillating for some, especially appealing for social conservatives and those who believe McCain's guy's screwed her last time around, but at the end of the day she simply cannot win and I believe she's smart enough to know it.

Here are five good reasons "Palin the Perky" should resist the temptation to jump into the deep end of a pool of GOP candidates that is still not fully formed:

1. Palin is limited: While she makes for good copy and assures that Tina Fey's career remains robust, Palin has shown us her stuff. She screeches, she's not all that articulate, and she still demonstrates

a limited ability to grasp the complexities of the country and the world. We've seen her fastball, her curve, and her slider. Unless she's holding a pitch we haven't seen, her range is limited.

2. Palin's base has too many choices: Bachmann, Paul, Gingrich, Santorum, Cain, and the likely entry of the twelve-thousand-pound gorilla himself, Rick Perry, mean social conservatives have too many choices. Palin's natural conservative base will be split in early contests. There is only so much of the base after Iowa, and New Hampshire is an open primary in which independents will play a big role. That means the Palin vote gets sliced and diced enough to allow her no significant plurality in important early states. Never mind that the GOP tends to nominate the candidate whose turn it is, and Palin loses that title to Mitt Romney this time.

3. Money: Palin has leveraged her commercial turn as the vice-presidential nominee into a lucrative career and a pretty respectable brand with a Fox News deal, a bestselling book, and big speaking fees. But running for President is not about making money; it's about raising money. While her Sarah PAC has raised some impressive cash as a support base, she will not be able to compete in raising the kinds of dollars she will need to win the nomination. No money, no message, no media! This is like playing "Deal Or No Deal." The dealer is offering more speaking fees, the chance to host your own show on Fox, multiple book deals, and maybe even the chance to fill in for Rush when he's on vacation or in rehab. Take the deal, Sarah! Take the deal!!

4. Sheer un-electability: While Sarah Palin is a great American, she cannot win a general election. She doesn't play well outside her comfort zone. (Pretty much from Skagway to Nome.) The GOP nominee must be able to hold the base and attract disenfranchised independents prepared to step away from President Obama's failed leadership on jobs and the economy. Sarah Palin is an easy caricature for the Democrats, and no matter how unpopular and vulnerable Barack Obama may be or might become, she does not attract independent voters. To attract those folks, she would need to step away from the very fringe that makes her so inviting to the hard

right of the Republican Party. Electability rarely trumps political ideology in a presidential primary, but this time Republicans MUST win. There is simply too much at stake.

5.  Campaigns are hard work! Sarah Palin knows well how uncomfortable a national campaign can be—and she only had to deal with it for a few months in 2008. Bad hotels, long periods away from home, grueling schedules, fast food, and of course, having to patiently entertain questions from all those Iowa and New Hampshire voters and then some. Then there's the mean old Main Stream Press: to be sure, some smart-aleck reporter might even have the unmitigated gall to ask her what she reads these days.

Governor Palin has made up her mind. And while only the Governor and her family know her exact plans, let us hope for the sake of the Republic and for the chance of a credible GOP nominee that she looks into the dark, cold water and decides it's much more comfortable to sit this one out comfortably poolside.

# STALEMATE:
## *Mired in the Muck*

I am a proud Republican. I am also someone who believes like most Americans that the process of legislative democracy is not easy or pretty. It is indeed, as someone once said, akin to making sausage. Most people like the way the stuff tastes, but if you see how it's made, you might quickly lose your appetite for that lumberjack breakfast.

So here we are, in the midst of a Washington stalemate on raising the nation's debt ceiling (again), and attempting to deal once and for all with the runaway government spending and deficits that most thinking people believe cannot be sustained. This not-so-pretty process has been paraded before the American people and the world as a passion play of political ideology in which both sides have painted themselves into a corner.

The House is expected to vote later today on House Speaker John Boehner's newest revision of "Cut, Cap, and Balance," which would effectively allow the debt ceiling to be raised in two steps provided that commensurate spending cuts are put into place. There's a little bit of everything in here for just about everyone not to like, but at the end of the day the bill achieves serious spending cuts in the first year and ensures that Congress can combat the President and the Democratic spend-a-holics' ability to continue to run up our collective national debt. Over the next ten years under Boehner's plan, spending would be reduced by over $900 billion! This is far better than the status quo, and a significant step forward given the political hand the Speaker has been dealt: Republicans controlling the House, Democrats in control of the

Senate, and the White House threatening a veto. In other words, the deal Boehner is putting forward for a House vote today is about the best we are going to get given the current environment and political structure of Washington.

Why, then, are Republicans choosing to eat their young by turning on the speaker? This is not just bad public policy and ridiculous politics. It's plain stupid. As *New Hampshire Union Leader* editorial director Drew Cline tweeted earlier today: "There would be no debt ceiling if there were no debt." The reality is that the only way to permanently and more effectively stop deficit spending and stop increasing the debt ceiling is to elect a Republican President and Republican majorities in both Houses. If Boehner's bill fails today, Republicans will have done nothing to advance that objective. In fact, they will only embolden President Obama and the Democrats, and likely make the President's re-election prospects stronger, by allowing him to point to the GOP as unable or unwilling to accept some compromise to protect a fragile economy and the full faith and credit of the United States. Imagine Barack Obama actually getting out of this election campaign without a scratch? He who has come to the table with no plan and no leadership and exhibited little more than the ability to whine from the bully pulpit on national television. If some reports on the negotiations are to be believed, he threw a hissy fit and walked out of at least one meeting held at The White House with congressional leaders. This guy is pathetic! The only thing more pathetic would be if the GOP summarily dismisses the best deal we are going to get, at least for now, by turning on the Speaker and in the process risking the bigger goal: to make President Obama a one-term wonder.

Mired in the muck is not an easy place to be. John Boehner has done his best to reach a compromise, but the pig-headed ideologues in his own party remain completely and totally intransigent. On the other side, liberal Democrats fueled by the Obama White House insist on extracting ever higher taxes from hard-working Americans—and yes Mr. President, that includes the middle class! Those of us who want a conservative government must remember another old adage: "Pigs get fat, hogs get slaughtered!"

# TROUBLE IN MAYBERRY:
## *The Don Knotts Presidency*

Remember Barney Fife? The lovable, bumbling, slightly neurotic and very nervous deputy to Andy Griffith's sheriff in the fictional town of Mayberry? *The Andy Griffith Show* was a television staple of the sixties, and represented a certain innocence that was quintessentially small-town America. There were no looting hoodlums or gangs, no terrorists or Muslim extremists bent on jihad, and no real need for serious law and order type leadership from the sheriff, the mayor, or the city council. Mayberry seemed to just chug right along. The biggest problem Deputy Barney Fife (portrayed by the late, great Don Knotts) had to deal with was an occasional vehicle illegally parked in front of Floyd's Barbershop, or Otis the town drunk's inability to let himself voluntarily into the cell at the police station because someone neglected to hang the key in its usual spot.

Knotts's character was nervous to the point of near-psychosis: almost always caught off-guard by even the most predictable of circumstances and about as clumsy as humanly conceivable. Barney Fife carried a gun with an empty chamber, but did keep a single bullet on his belt—just in case. He crashed the squad car, misplaced bail money, and even managed to misunderstand a call to the station from a concerned citizen informing him that a person named Martin was coming to town. When Barney heard "Martin" as "Martians," you can imagine the comic premise and general anxiety that ensued. Barney Fife was about as ill-prepared to deal with legitimately enforcing the law in Mayberry as Barack Obama has proven himself to be in leading the United States of America. I know that's harsh, but consider the following.

Let us consider the pratfalls of the Obama presidency to date: when he took office, promising "Hope and Change," unemployment had climbed to nearly 7.6%. The new sheriff made fast work of that, claiming he would create jobs. Today, the jobless rate stands well over 8.5%. The community-organizer-in-chief said taxes would not be raised on a single American outside of the wealthiest ONE percent. Turns out the wealthiest one percent are largely small businesses, many family run, LLCs, and partnerships—that means middle-class folks who employ real people in the private sector. It's actually funny to hear the President continue to refer to these people as "private jet owners" or "the wealthiest one percent."

Spending has been a problem and to be fair, President Bush deserves his share of blame for increasing the size and scope of government. But Obama came to Mayberry and "Fifed" the debt to nearly 95% of our GDP. The next foible was a trillion-dollar stimulus plan that would create "shovel-ready" jobs, which flopped so incredibly that the President's party was summarily thrown out of office in the 2010 midterm elections to allow Republicans a clear majority in the House and near-majority in the Senate. Conflicts continue to rage overseas, Guantanamo is still open for business, and the debt ceiling debacle has earned the President the distinction of being the first President in the history of the republic to preside over a downgrade in America's credit rating from one of the major credit rating agencies. The Chinese hold us hostage by manipulating their currency and killing domestic manufacturing. Violence has broken out across Europe. Oh and let us not forget, the President is still crowing about his plans to turn nearly one sixth of our domestic economy over to the federal government so they can reform health care!

That means the same folks who have all but bankrupted Social Security and Medicare, who provide that friendly assistance over at the IRS, and who now have put the U.S. Postal System on life support are now going to be responsible for putting U.S. on life support? This guy is making many Americans yearn for the salad days of Herbert Hoover!

Alas, all is not well in Mayberry. The President's failure to lead, and his inability to grasp the fundamental concepts of market capitalism and entrepreneurship as essential American means toward a successful and healthy economy, are examples of his clumsy Don Knotts behavior. This President, like Barney Fife, is patently unprepared and unable to do his job. His failure to lead would be funny, like Deputy Fife's inability to truly maintain law and order in bucolic Mayberry. Unfortunately, we're not in Mayberry anymore!

The President appears clueless, unprepared, inept, and more than a little bit nervous at a time when real leadership is needed more than ever at the federal level. Instead of offering solutions, he storms out of meetings with congressional leadership in a snit. Instead of presenting real ideas for job creation and debt reduction, he says "Everything's on the table" and waits for someone else to present him a plan. Instead of offering his own ideas, he whines at press conferences, asking for the partisan bickering in Washington to stop. Instead of stepping forward, calling Congress back to Washington to settle this mess, he's packing for his annual vacation to Fantasy Island (aka Martha's Vineyard) to wring his hands with the like-minded anti-capitalists and "beautiful people that inhabit Oak Bluffs and Edgartown." Please pass the Beluga! Fantasy Island indeed!

The difference between President Obama and Barney Fife is this: when it came to a crisis, at least Barney had a gun and a bullet if he needed it. He was at least arguably somewhat prepared. The President has nothing. Nada. Zero. Zilch. Crickets. And there's simply nothing funny about that.

# IT'S THEIR FAULT:
*Axelrod says "Blame the guys across the aisle!"*

Presidential political guru David Axelrod is a smart guy. I was looking forward to hearing his take on the 2012 campaign and some early and potentially brilliant new insights that might form the narrative for the President's 2012 re-election campaign. The New Hampshire Institute of Politics at St. Anselm College packed the house for "The Ax Man" recently. Democrats sat collectively on the edge of their seats, waiting for the guru who essentially wrote the "Hope and Change" screenplay for the 2008 Obama campaign to come up with something encouraging and thoughtful: a road map for the next four years. The faithful, however, were very much let down.

The mood in the room seemed confused, depressed and slightly despondent. Maybe because that's the way Axelrod presented his case for Obama redux.

David Axelrod is a low-key fellow—no James Carville is he! Mild mannered, he looks more like a guy who's shown up to perform a tax audit than to win you the White House. One need only to watch a segment of him on any given Sunday morning talk show to see that he is understated to the point of almost anesthetizing! But understated and smart are not mutually exclusive. For that reason, while what he says might be low-key, it is usually thoughtful and worth listening to. What I heard was an unenergetic thud that played in the room much like I suspect it will play with voters come November 2012. The problem according to Axelrod: those "diabolically" successful Republicans whose single stated *raison d'être* is to defeat the President. There was more: "It's all Bush's fault," "We inherited it," "Republicans are solely politically motivated," and on and on...*ZZZZZZZZ*.

There was nothing new. No new narrative, no hint at a message that would inspire the faithful to stay with the President. No preview to the second chapter, the chance to finish what he has begun in earnest. The guy at the next table actually nodded off briefly and I know for a fact he's a Democrat!

The point is, Axelrod left the people who are already opposed to Obama's policies convinced that the administration is not only out of effective ideas to turn the economy around, but also out of a cogent political narrative for another term. Even the local union rep politely asked when he "and his guys" might expect some jobs—suggesting perhaps maybe a little trouble even with the base.

Axelrod launched a solid attack on special interests and Super PACs. He's opposed to all that money in politics. But the President will raise and spend over a billion dollars on his own re-election campaign. And since when did Super PACs or special interests weighing in on elections become the exclusive problem of Republicans? A question on the role of independent voters in the election was met with "People need to decide for themselves" and "I have faith they will make the right decision." With all due respect, a lot of independents have made that decision already.

I respect Axelrod the campaign master, "The Guru," but his prescription for the Democratic base was, in a word, anemic. Perhaps in the weeks and months to come Mr. Axelrod and a few of those pro-Obama Super PACs will come up with a better message than "It's not our fault." Something tells me the only strategy they may have is to make the GOP nominee an unacceptable alternative to the President. The politically scientific term for that is known as: winning ugly!

# DROPPING LIKE A ROCK:
## *The Perry Problem*

Just when things seemed like they couldn't get much worse for Texas Governor Rick Perry's presidential campaign, they did. A couple of poor debate performances, the "Ponzi scheme" language in reference to social security, the poor showing in a couple of completely meaningless straw polls. Now, a conservative base that should be all his is nervous about his "path to citizenship" position and in-state tuition discounts for illegals in Texas. Add to all this a new problem: the "N" word!

According to a Washington Post report, Perry owned a land lease in Middle of Nowhere, Texas, where visitors were greeted at the property's entrance by a large rock which boasted the property's name as... well, let's just say it allegedly contained the "N" word. Yikes!

Regardless of whether the "sources" the *Washington Post* quotes as having actually seen the offending boulder are telling the truth, the whole thing adds to the one argument establishment Republicans have been using against Perry as the GOP nominee since he arrived at this prom: his electability.

In fairness, the Perry people claim the offending rock was "painted over," and then at some later point it was actually turned face down so as not to be seen. I'm not sure how big this meteorite actually is, but were I Rick Perry I think I might have suggested that after the thing was painted over it be dynamited and removed from his hunting land completely, totally, and absolutely. One would also think that someone on the Governor's staff might have been in touch with the owners of the leased land to suggest they might want to change the name of the place and the deed and any other Texas property records, mailing lists, or references to the old, inappropriate, and offensive name. Painting over it is, well, wimpier than I would expect from a guy like Perry. Any guy who can shoot a coyote while jogging should have no trouble dealing with a rock!

The Perry situation plays to type. It may not be fair, but it is true. Republicans smell the chance at victory against a weakened and ineffectual incumbent President whose policies have nearly bankrupted the country. Why nominate a candidate who is not ready for prime time, a candidate who could be difficult to sell to America? Grabbing defeat from the jaws of victory is not a new concept for Republicans, but it simply will not be tolerated this time around.

Rick Perry could be one good debate away from rebuilding his image, but he also needs to make sure he is ready to face the President in a national general election. The land lease ruckus adds to the uncertainty of Perry vs. Obama, and may just cause Perry's poll numbers to continue to drop...just like a rock!

★

# CHAPTER SEVEN

# SUPERMAN IN BIFOCALS:
## *New Hampshire's Bill Gardner to the Rescue!*

We all know by now that the folks down in Disney World (aka Florida) have decided, against the expressed rules of the Republican National Committee, to move Florida's primary ahead to January 31, 2012. We've heard it all before. "We want a more significant role." "Why should New Hampshire be first?" Yada, yada, yada. Now what we have is a small but interesting scrum as early primary states begin to jockey their own primary dates ahead of Florida. As of this moment, the likely calendar appears as follows: the Iowa caucus moves up to the first week in January, followed by the New Hampshire primary exactly seven days later. South Carolina has announced a move to January 21 and Nevada will follow it by a few days. It is important to note that the AARP crowd in Florida has accomplished exactly nothing by creating this circus stunt. They who first illustrated to the world that they could not punch a "hanging chad" forcefully enough to go through a butterfly ballot and effectively cast a vote in the 2000 presidential campaign will still remain exactly fourth in the succession of nominating states. And while the net result may push a few more visitors through the already endless lines at Splash Mountain, exactly what this accomplishes for the Little Miss Sunshine State remains a mystery to me. It does screw up a lot of campaigns whose travel, logistics, and budgeting have been planned for a long time (unless, of course, you're Chris Christie!)

One thing nobody should underestimate is the ironclad resolve of one Bill Gardner, New Hampshire's diminutive Secretary of State. Gardner takes his role in upholding New Hampshire's "First in the Nation" status pretty seriously. This is nothing new for Gardner.

States have been claiming for years that New Hampshire shouldn't be first; that the state is too small, too white, and too cold to be the first primary. Gardner, however, remains undeterred, and simply reminds people every four years that New Hampshire law requires that the state's presidential primary be held at least seven days before any "similar contest." I am convinced that if Gardner needed to hold the primary during the halftime of the Thanksgiving Day bowl games, he could manage it without a problem. The First in the Nation Primary has become one of the great traditions of American politics. In addition, New Hampshire is a small enough state (and media market) for a number of lesser-known candidates to actually compete— or at least attempt to be heard. New Hampshire is also pretty used to all this. In the tradition of annual town meetings, the residents of the Granite State have become generationally trained to participate in the primary process. They vote, attend political town halls and meet-the-candidate nights, and engage in extended and sometimes intimate discussions with those who would be President at endless house parties. I still marvel at those New Hampshire citizens who are unfazed by cameras, network news stars, and packed rooms. They refuse to be intimidated while asking tough questions publicly, even insisting on specific follow-ups from the candidates if not satisfied with their answers.

Once again, Bill Gardner comes to the rescue calmly, without a lot of fanfare or real concern. He has moved the candidate filing dates up to October 17th from the 28th. He patiently fields media inquiries about what all this will mean without ever getting terribly fazed or even showing the slightest bit of annoyance at all the national committee infighting. Gardner, like New Hampshire itself, is a reminder of why this state is so reliable when it comes to conducting fair, open, and engaged primary contests.

Gardner's demeanor is all Clark Kent, but his past performance is all Superman. When it comes to ensuring New Hampshire's First in the Nation status, he remains faster than a speeding motorcade, more powerful than a Florida party boss, able to leap over would-be ambitious interlopers in a single bound. In short, Bill Gardner simply cannot and will not be deterred—even by the Kryptonite-like moves of states like Florida—from his goals of upholding truth, justice, and the New Hampshire way!

Mickey Mouse might be a big deal. But he and all the palm trees, bad drivers, and blue-haired retirees from the sunshine state combined are simply no threat to New Hampshire as long as Bill Gardner's in charge!

## HUNTING SEASON:
### *Huntsman Camps Out in NH, But Will He Hunt?*

"That dog won't hunt." We've all heard that expression regarding an approach, an idea, a scheme, a product, or even a presidential candidate. I've heard more than one political insider suggest that phrase applies to former Utah Governor and Ambassador to China Jon Huntsman. On paper, he's an impressive candidate: Governor, ambassador, Deputy Assistant Secretary of Commerce, CEO of a large family corporation. But over the years, a number of candidates who certainly had the experience to be President simply never caught on and couldn't raise the money. Their campaigns ended long before Super Tuesday. Some have ended the day after New Hampshire.

This appears to be the case with Huntsman. Every person I talk to who has met the Governor or attended one of his campaign events is impressed. They say, "He's much better one-on-one," "He's smart and likeable," and "I think he could beat Obama in a general election." The problem is, right now there appears to be a real disconnect between Huntsman the person and Huntsman the brand in the race for the White House. New Hampshire is a small state and predisposed to the kind of retail campaigning that Huntsman does so well. But Jon Huntsman simply cannot shake hands with every voter in the state. Unless he can find a way to connect with more Granite State voters *en masse,* his road to the White House ends here.

Huntsman has essentially staked everything he has left on New Hampshire, closing down his Florida campaign headquarters and committing all resources to a place where his campaign feels he might be able to stake a claim on more moderate Republicans and Independents. This strategy rarely works. John McCain chose not to play in Iowa in 2000, and spent all of his time and much of his treasure riding the "Straight Talk Express" from one end of New Hampshire to the other—ultimately clobbering (my then-client) George W. Bush. But a New Hampshire victory without a subsequent bounce in subsequent contests rings pretty hollow. The primaries are now earlier and bunched tightly together. Candidates need national money and staff to pivot from one state to another. Even if Huntsman were to upset the better-known, better-funded national candidates like Mitt Romney and Rick Perry here, few believe he could turn his brand of Republicanism into a political narrative that would play in conservative South Carolina or Florida and put him in real contention.

The real role Jon Huntsman plays while camping out here in New Hampshire may be as an unwitting player in the Romney/Perry scrum. Huntsman, I believe, takes more votes from Romney here than he does from Perry. Should he catch on, Huntsman could become the voice of reason, a thinking man's Republican, and an alternative to the conventional wisdom of Romney or Perry. Should Huntsman begin to connect here with voters, he would become the Perry campaign's best hope of taking it to Romney in what is essentially the former Massachusetts Governor's home state. The stakes for Romney are high here, and the Perry folks like their chances of bracketing New Hampshire with strong showings (if not outright wins) in the socially conservative bookends of Iowa and South Carolina. It's a Texas sized strategy—let's see if it works.

A "real" Huntsman in New Hampshire could be Romney's worst nightmare. Independent expenditures will pour into the state. While some may attempt to define Perry, my sense is that more will attempt to negatively define Romney. An air and ground war between the GOP titans would only help Huntsman.

The other thing I find fascinating is the media's fawning over Huntsman. They see him as more mainstream and smart. He's well-suited for their version of what they think the GOP nominee should be. They wonder aloud to one another on Twitter and in the blogosphere why the rest of us just don't seem to get it.

The real answer is simple: the press doesn't pick the nominee, and what they see is very different from what the engaged GOP voter sees in the early contests. Huntsman's ability to stay in the race depends almost entirely on whether or not he "hunts" in New Hampshire.

He has assembled some good staffers here: a terrific pollster in my old pal Whit Ayres and an army of couch-surfing college-age volunteers who are working hard on the ground game. Jon Huntsman has staked everything he has in this race on his success in New Hampshire, and one never knows. Maybe, just maybe, it could work. Then again… maybe not.

Happy hunting, Governor!

# CHAPTER NINE

# IT'S GETTING UGLIER THAN A STEPSISTER OUT THERE:
### *Countdown to the Ultimate Test of Romney/ Perry Electability, and Get Ready to Rumble!*

New polling data released in the past couple of days suggests what we have all known for a while: former Massachusetts Governor Mitt Romney remains the front runner in the race for the GOP nomination... at least for now.

Polling from Quinnipiac shows Romney with 22% of the vote, Herman Cain with 17%, and Perry down to 14%. Similar results are reflected in other national polling, including a CBS poll that ties Romney and Herman Cain with 17% each, while Rick Perry trails with 12%. Remember that these are national polls. Frankly, they mean little to the political narrative, which will unfold based on the actual results of Iowa, New Hampshire, and other early contests. Political campaigns are to be measured far more carefully in early primary states. Momentum and beating expectations lead to more campaign cash, media coverage, and candidate visibility. In the coming days UNH pollster Andrew Smith will release his findings in New Hampshire, and next week a new poll conducted by the Institutes of Politics at St. Anselm College and Harvard's Kennedy School will give us another sneak peek at what Granite Staters are thinking.

One might concur that all this is good news for Romney. I would agree except for two potential problems that are about to become political reality. Chuck Todd, NBC's political director, reported this morning that Perry's fundraising for the third quarter will be an impressive $17 million, just a tad less than Romney will have raised during the same period. Perry also has a nice little Christmas club of some $15 million on hand and ready to go to work, presumably on Romney in Iowa and New Hampshire. Anyone who has followed Perry's successful gubernatorial races in Texas will tell you that he and his advisors are not afraid to run what some have called a scorched-earth campaign—meaning they are not timid about defining their opponents. Expect big dollars from Perry and Perry-friendly Super PACs to begin the carpet-bombing any day now in an attempt to paint Romney as an unacceptable nominee, especially for the conservative base who already has some reservations about him. The Perry folks see Romney as a soft frontrunner with a glass jaw on a number of key issues they feel will peel his support away faster than you can say "Obamney-Care."

Team Perry might also invest some of that Texas campaign cash in a debate coach, which could pay off for the boss in the next round of debates. As lackluster as Perry's first appearances were, he is just one good debate away from rewriting his next act and quite possibly staging a comeback that could change things overnight. The real questions are whether Romney's brand can handle the incoming artillery and whether he will counterattack. If this thing starts to get messy, both campaigns will have no shortage of cash to burn down the village. This kind of campaign ultimately only benefits the current occupant of the White House. My bet for now is that people in New Hampshire know Romney better. They view him as more electable, and therefore they will likely stick with him. This is not necessarily the case in Iowa and South Carolina, where a credible social conservative will likely do well.

Iowans and Granite Staters are already bracing for the onslaught: not answering land lines (those pesky pollsters), duct-taping their mailboxes shut, and upping their spam filters just enough to protect their already-overflowing electronic inboxes. With Michelle Bachmann nearly out of the race, Cain without the money to really play on the national stage, Christie out (yes, folks, he said it: "No means no until it's a yes"), Congressman Ron Paul with nowhere to go beyond his maximum 15-point ceiling, and the rest of the candidates simply unremarkable enough at this point to even make a credible case for a national campaign, this thing remains a Romney/Perry wrestling match at least for now. To be sure, the Mitt Romney and Rick Perry that voters in Iowa and New Hampshire will see in a month from now will likely be very different than the candidates they know today. The candidate who has the credibility to weather the media storm will win the primary. In the meantime, be careful where you step. Scorched earth can really burn your feet!

★

# CHAPTER TEN

# MEET THE "HERMINATOR":
## *15 Reasons Herman Cain is Cool*

I know this race is between Mitt Romney and Rick Perry, at least for now. Right? Wrong! While Romney remains the clear frontrunner for the GOP nomination, by all accounts Perry continues his precipitous slide. Sure, in the national polls, it's all Romney and Perry. Problem is, those polls don't matter a whit! We are 11 months away from a general election, so what folks in Tennessee and Idaho think is not so important right now. In the early contests of Iowa, New Hampshire, and South Carolina, voters will have the chance to begin to winnow the field. And right now, based on what I've been seeing and hearing, there's a guy to watch out there who has the momentum and the message potential to surprise a lot of people in the early contests: Herman Cain. You know him as the successful businessman and tell-it-to-you-straight-up guy who is passionate, funny and frankly more Ronald Reagan than anyone else in the GOP pack right now.

Cain brings a fresh and genuine conservative perspective and an articulate authenticity to the race that is interesting, compelling, and, I think, growing on people in Iowa and New Hampshire and across the country. On top of all of that, you have to admire his uniquely American success story and the fact that he's about as self-made as they come. This guy embodies the American dream. Even though he has never been in politics before, he commands a presence, and part of it is a clear and unequivocal sense of what he believes in his heart. I'm not endorsing Herman Cain—I won't endorse any candidate in this race, at least for now—but I must admit part of me can't help but root for him just a bit. Each time I watch his debate performances or see him interviewed,

I find myself compelled to listen. I want to learn more. The thing every candidate really needs at this stage is the ability to make voters listen. So now that I've told you I like the guy and that I think he's catching on, let me share with you the 15 reasons I think he's a good candidate and why I see Mr. Cain moving up in the polls in the days and weeks to come. He just may have a shot at surprising more than a few of the chattering class in Washington as the first votes in Iowa and New Hampshire begin to be counted. I call it the "Cain Cool Factor." I know, I know what you're saying, he's never run for elective office before and he has no shot. That's likely true. Novices make mistakes and Mr. Cain will likely make his share. But for now at least, here's why he's definitely cool:

1.  He has an amazing amount of experience with some pretty impressive corporations, including Coca-Cola USA, Burger King, and its parent Pillsbury. He is best known as the President and CEO of Godfather's Pizza. (This guy clearly knows a good slice!)

2.  Love the jamming rock/country anthem he uses on web videos, including my all-time favorite, "Get on Board the Herman Cain Train!"

3.  He has got a great set of pipes! That voice was custom-made for the presidency. (Think of the fortune America will save by not needing a sound system for a President Cain inaugural speech!)

4.  He stole the Olympic torch icon from Romney for his "Cain for President" graphic.

5.  His positions sound more like Reagan than Reagan. On the economy: Feds tax too much, spend too much, and he effectively pushes the case for meaningful tax reform now. Alternative energy sources are important, but these solutions must come by reducing regulations and encouraging private-sector companies to take the lead on innovating new energy solutions. If alternative energy sources are inexpensive, safe, and plentiful, American consumers will choose to purchase them. On healthcare: America needs patient-centered healthcare reform. Allow the deductibility of health insurance

premiums whether they are paid for by business or consumers. On immigration: secure the borders, enforce our laws, and promote the existing path to citizenship. On national security: strengthen it. This guy's The Gipper incarnate!

6. He has great rhetorical skills, which also remind me (just a little) of Reagan. Here are a few of his lines: "We can and we must turn this nation around." "There is no greater force on earth than the united will of the American people." "America: the sleeping giant has been awakened!" "America will not compromise her legacy. She will not accept debt or mediocrity." "Empowerment, not entitlement."

7. He has the 9-9-9 plan to restructure the tax system (9% flat tax, 9% business flat tax, 9% national sales tax—everything else goes). If the 9-9-9 tax plan doesn't work for him, it would make a great Godfather's promotion: for a limited time, 9 toppings before 9pm for $9. Good concept!

8. He wears cool bright yellow neckties.

9. He keeps using the phrase "Let's get real" during presidential debates. Appropriate, especially after a Ron Paul rant!

10. He has great campaign "swag" available for sale on his website.

11. The man's a stage 4 cancer survivor. This dude's a fighter!

12. He keeps talking about some Chilean model. Not sure who she is, but he mentions her a lot. I'm assuming she must be hot!

13. He has a cool Twitter handle, @THEHermancain.

14. He talks a lot about his mom and dad, his wife, his kids, and his grandkids.

15. He will make China nervous.

Keep an eye on Herman Cain. If he doesn't become President, here's my plug for Commerce Secretary or better yet, VP. Republicans could possibly do a lot worse than Herman Cain, and from what I can tell, they're starting to realize it. For whatever it's worth, Herman Cain is a man on the move! Most importantly he's way cooler than the rest of the pack. At least for now. No mistakes Mr. Cain, the voters are starting to take notice!

# THE SCORE DOESN'T MATTER IN THE FIRST INNING:
*Everything Looks Fine… Until It Doesn't!*

Monday was a good day for Mitt Romney in New Hampshire. He held a couple of town hall meetings and rolled out the support of one of the most popular politicians the Granite State has ever produced, U.S. Senator Judd Gregg. The day got even better mid-day, when the New Hampshire Institute of Politics at St. Anselm College, in partnership with the Institute of Politics at Harvard, released its latest presidential primary poll. The poll of 648 likely New Hampshire voters was conducted from October 2nd to 6th by John Della Volpe, director of polling for Harvard's Institute of Politics. The good news for Mitt: he continues to lead the GOP field with 38%. Nothing new. Romney has been the frontrunner in New Hampshire since he announced his campaign.

The real news of the poll was twofold. First, Texas Governor Rick Perry received just 4% of the vote, leaving him in single digits along with Jon Huntsman, Michelle Bachmann, Rick Santorum, Gary Johnson, and Newt Gingrich. Texas congressman Ron Paul placed third with 13%. But that's not the big news. The big news is that 20% of those polled indicated they would support businessman Herman Cain. The Cain surge has been reported in a number of local and national polls over the last ten days. Cain has won a couple of straw polls, and his rhetoric on the Occupy Wall Street movement, decrying the President for promoting class warfare, has struck many as the straightest talk they've heard in a while. What's more, Cain's 9-9-9 plan to overhaul the tax system may be a bit dodgy to some who think it simply won't work, but it's a plan that's fast becoming a recognizable brand—and one Cain talks about incessantly these days.

So what does this all mean? Given the now compressed dates of early caucus and primary contests, and with New Hampshire possibly holding its primary on Halloween (I fear), there's not a lot of time left for the dynamic to swing a whole lot. I know, things change, and the last thing anyone wants to be is the frontrunner in New Hampshire this far from when Iowa even votes. But one also senses that right now may be the calm before the storm. The twists and turns ahead in the presidential nomination process are uncharted. We'll no doubt be surprised again and again before the nomination is wrapped up. Herman's up now, but is he ready for the challenges he faces as he unexpectedly starts to appear as a possible threat? Watch out Mr. Cain: frontrunners don't like upstart challengers! As the Boy Scouts say: Be Prepared!

Today, the Perry campaign released a viral video attacking Romney as a carbon copy of Obama. While that claim is clearly a stretch, Romney has yet to face strong negative messaging. It appears Perry is ready to begin some definition, which may peel away some of that frontrunner patina.

Other findings of the poll were:

- 78% of those polled (likely Republican primary voters) believed that if the general election were held today and Mitt Romney were the GOP nominee, he would defeat Barack Obama.

- 65% reported that they were satisfied with the current group of Republican candidates.

- 7% believed the country is heading in the right direction, while 89% believe it is off on the wrong track.

Mr. President: you have a problem! As a number of national pundits have pointed out this past week, there is plenty of time for these numbers to change. But this is an interesting snapshot of where the candidates stand now, at least in the minds of NH voters.

Things are far from settled in the Granite State, but the stakes couldn't be higher for tonight's Dartmouth/*Washington Post*/WBIN-TV debate in Hanover. Keep your eyes on Romney, Cain, and Perry in that order. These guys may actually make a little news tonight because there's still plenty at stake in New Hampshire.

# LIGHTS, CAMERA, ACTION:
### *Was Tuesday Night at Dartmouth the Beginning of a Cinderella Story?*

On Tuesday night in Hanover, NH, it was as if Hollywood had invaded this bucolic New Hampshire town to shoot a movie about a debate that took place on an Ivy League campus. The fall foliage was at its peak, the media trucks, with their satellite uplinks and key lights were strategically set to create a pure New Hampshire backdrop for the stand-up talking heads from the networks and their affiliates. In the middle of it all was what can only be described as a small open circus tent, complete with raised staging, a full television lighting grid, and multiple cameras. This was Bloomberg Television's "Debate Central," from where its pundits and prognosticators would preach the bible of political interpretation as if the debating candidates would be speaking in Farsi.

In the middle of this menagerie, with unseasonably warm temperatures in the seventies, Dartmouth students threw Frisbees and wandered around the green to various stakeouts trying to discern who exactly was speaking to the camera. "That's Chris Christie, the Governor of New Jersey," one kid told a group of friends in Tuck School of Business sweatshirts. On this, the balmiest of October weekends in many a year, the Bloomberg TV/ *Washington Post* / WBIN-TV GOP presidential debate pre-game was unfolding. AIDS activists chanted from the steps of the Dartmouth Student Center. A guy with several iPhones mounted on a helmet, wearing a white rubber raincoat and carrying two laptops beaming instant data of some type (perhaps from the mother ship), circulated through the crowd. One woman stood behind me as I prepared to do a live on-camera interview with a hand-painted sign that read

"KEEP YOUR POLITICS OUT OF MY UTERUS!" I assured her just before I went on that she needn't worry—I would.

Even the Occupy Wall Street crowd made it to the circus, with signs that said things like "I'm NOT the RICHEST 1%'s ATM," and one of my particular favorites: a twenty-something gentlemen held a placard which read: "Not Showering Until Wall Street Crumbles." Clever and effective. This guy was committed to the cause and his personal hygiene testified to the fact that he had been at the cause for a while now. Standing near him for just a moment, I actually felt Wall Street crumbling might not be such a bad thing if it got this guy to shower.

Sideshow aside, the real action was about to begin inside Moore Theater. The seven GOP candidates (sans Buddy Roemer and Gary Johnson, who were excluded) were about to seat themselves around Charlie Rose's famous wooden table (he of PBS fame) and take two hours of questions focused solely on the economy. Bloomberg has cleverly positioned 2012 as the "economy election," not only because of the importance of jobs and the economy to voters, but also because the economy, jobs, and financial news are the network's area of segmented cable expertise. I imagine if ESPN decided to cover the campaign they might label 2012 as "The Next Round Draft Pick Election." In any event, I sat high in the balcony of the adjoining media filing center. My old pal Alex Castellanos from CNN joined me, along with my colleague Nate Grimes from GY&K. We were ready to live-Tweet, and Tweet we did.

The debate itself can be summed up as follows: Mitt Romney and Herman Cain kept reciting the numbers 9-9-9. They had most of the juice. Perry pretty much called in his debate performance and proved in a couple of cutaway shots that he either had no interest in the event, or he was mildly sedated. Senator Rick Santorum was about the feistiest I've seen him. He tried to hit the Herminator's 9-9-9 tax plan by asking the audience if they really wanted a 9% sales tax. (A slightly loaded question, given the Granite State has NO sales or income tax.) Michelle Bachmann was solid and kept referring to herself as a former federal tax lawyer. I believe that's a fancy way to say she worked for the

IRS. Professor Newt Gingrich, perfectly at home at Dartmouth, was his usual smart/lecturing self. And Jon Huntsman, the former Utah Governor and Ambassador to China, was there with more comedy material. He attempted a religious joke at the expense of Rick Perry (referencing that one creepy pastor supporter of his who referred to Mormonism as a "cult"). He also joked about Cain's plan sounding like a pizza deal. Thankfully, he then stopped the stand-up act and started debating.

Romney won. Period. End of story. Cain was solid, funny, and engaging. Everyone else should have simply stayed out on the Green and joined the undergrads in Frisbee. There were no real changes here, but things are still interesting. Romney is the frontrunner, but Cain is surging while Perry is sinking. Paul is holding his zany but devoted followers and will take about 15% of the vote on the day of the New Hampshire primary. But does all this even matter right now? Romney appears to be a soft frontrunner. We will soon see how soft when Perry begins a much-anticipated nuclear winter of negative advertising designed to take the shine off Romney pretty fast. The problem is, driving up Romney's negative image and eroding his ballot support does not necessarily drive voters to Perry. And Perry and his Super PAC have yet to really light up the airwaves.

Cain must prove that he and his 9-9-9 plan are more than just a book tour. He will need to build on his plan and provide additional details and somehow tangibly demonstrate that it will work to reform the tax code, cut taxes, and balance the budget. If he does not, 9-9-9 could be the 2012 version of the Steve Forbes flat tax proposal, which some will recall made Forbes a short-lived nerdy rock star in the 1996 campaign until it fizzled under the glare of economists who tagged it as a pure gimmick.

And then there's this: if not Cain or Perry (and certainly not Ron Paul), who becomes the alternative to Mitt Romney? There's always one, and be sure there will be again. One of the supporting players will begin the slow ascent toward challenging the conventional wisdom. It would be a come-from-behind Cinderella story, the kind of thing you see in those Hollywood movies shot in dramatic style in the perfect setting, very much like the one at Dartmouth College Tuesday night. Maybe even the feisty Rick Santorum on display this night at The Dartmouth Debate would somehow emerge from the shadows to mount a challenge to Romney Inc. Stranger things have happened.

# CHAPTER THIRTEEN

# DUDE, CAN YOU SPARE A DIME:
## *The Day I Occupied Wall Street (in Boston)*

Late last week, I took my dogs Rocky and Fenway for a morning walk from my Back Bay apartment, up through Downtown Crossing, and into the Financial District. I had been reading and watching the goings-on here in Boston, New York, and across the country since the rise of the "Occupy Wall Street" protests—an effort that had produced among other things some of the craziest Loons ever assembled to collectively grumble about anything. I decided I had to experience for myself their passion and commitment to stopping forever the corporate greed—nay, capitalism itself—from destroying our republic. I knew there were a bunch of these "patriots" camping out in plastic tents (they call them "bungalows") along the newly beautified Rose Kennedy Greenway, and that they had been seen in various parts of the city looking for whatever they perceived to be ill-gotten capitalistic gain at work. Having experienced three of their legion up close and personal, I'm surprised they weren't conducting a sit-in in front of a Bank of America ATM!

As I walked into Boston's financial district, I could see the crowd (what they call the "General Assembly") up further toward Dewey Square. I was going to march right into the belly of the beast to feel it, sense it, and smell it all for myself, but before I could get much closer I ran into three guys who were holding a "pre-protest" just before the actual protest. (Think of them as the coming attraction before the main feature.) I was face-to-face with three young gentlemen who were only too happy to be interviewed by a middle-aged member of the wealthiest one percent.

"What's going on up here?" I asked.

"It's the General Assembly. You know, OWS?" said a guy who looked to be in his mid-twenties. He was wearing a green army jacket with patch on the collar bearing (of all things) a hammer and sickle.

"I thought the General Assembly was in New York," I said, "at the UN?"

All three laughed at me. I'm not certain they knew what the UN in New York actually was.

Rocky, my Portuguese Water Dog, earnestly sniffed at Army Jacket's retro Chuck Taylor Converse high-tops, the tongues of which were hanging loosely under their untied rainbow laces.

"Occupy Wall Street, dude," said another twenty-something sporting a pink-tinged faux hawk, who introduced himself only as Chad.

"Oh, what's up with that?" I asked casually. I had prepared for this assignment by donning jeans, an untucked polo shirt, and an old and very pilled Patagonia fleece vest along with one of my oldest Red Sox caps. They'd never suspect I was the enemy!

Army Jacket looked at me as though I had sprouted a second head. "We're taking our country back!" he said, a little too enthusiastically.

Chad lit a cigarette and took a long pull. "America's really screwed," he said, shaking his head. I noted Chad and Jacket were both drinking Starbucks beverages and made a mental note to re-check the cost of a Venti the next time I stopped in for a cup. My first reaction to the familiar white and green cups was that these guys should have an issue with any corporate coffee giant that made a profit and had obligations to its shareholders.

"I know," I agreed. "You think Obama's in trouble?"

Army Jacket said, "Obama's not the problem. It's the banks and the rich. They get bailed out, we get sold out!" I'd heard this line in every piece of protest video I'd seen from these guys! I was hoping for something more original.

"You need new lines," I offered.

The other kid, who never gave his name, stood with a hand-lettered sign. It read "Prosperity over Profits." I thought about that. In a Romney-esque moment my Republican capitalist brain urged me to say, "Prosperity comes from profits, stupid!" But I held my tongue, as there was no sense blowing my cover. It seemed this guy's sole assignment was holding the sign up to the traffic jam amassing in front of us in order to get people to wave, honk, or proffer him the finger. From what I observed, he was getting a variety of all these reactions. Each made him hoot and holler like an over-served Bruins fan in the final period.

"You guys go to school in Boston?" I asked matter-of-factly, as three Boston police cruisers roared by us, sirens blaring, headed toward the General Assembly.

"We do," Chad and Army Jacket said in semi-unison.

"Really? Where do you go?" I asked.

Chad said, "Emerson." That seemed to fit.

Jacket went to MIT. At the risk of being accused of profiling, he didn't strike me as MIT material. But he could have been studying chemical and biological anarchy, which would have made perfect sense. I made another mental note to find out what MIT considered acceptable GPA and SAT scores for admission these days. Maybe they had dropped their standards?

The kid with the sign started yelping, "We're the 99%!" Rocky began barking excitedly with him, which seemed to animate him even more. "Your dog digs the movement," he said.

Chad stopped giggling at the kid with the sign and he and Jacket began patiently to try to make me understand.

"Country's all effed up 'cause of the banks," said Jacket. "The banks are screwing us."

"Yeah," I agreed. "They keep raising the ATM rates and there's never any place to park."

He ignored me.

"The rich get richer and there's no jobs for the rest of us," Chad said earnestly.

"And are the rich the ones who aren't hiring?" I asked. (It's hard for a guy like me not to be a smartass, even when working undercover.)

"Corporate profits are at an all-time high, dude," said Jacket. This was the second time he had referred to me as "dude," which I took as a compliment. Until now I believed I was too old to be a dude. I was slightly flattered.

"The rich make all the money and keep it for themselves," Chad added.

The kid with the sign went bouncing after a couple of Boston cops on horseback, jumping and hollering like a kid who'd just seen his first pony.

"He's a little excited," I observed.

"He's all about it," said Chad. "Maybe he should cut back on the Red Bull," I suggested. No response just collective laughing.

 "His dad's here too, works for the union," offered Jacket.

"The union?" I asked acting dumbfounded. "Western Union?"

They again laughed loudly.

"The Union Pacific Railroad?" I tried again.

They continued their collective guffawing. "SEIW," said Chad. "We're all hooked up in this thing."

"Union activity? I'm shocked. Shocked, I tell you." I laughed at this line, because neither Chad nor Jacket appreciated the Casablanca reference. At least I get a kick out of myself. "What do you guys think of Obama?" I asked, walking slowly up the sidewalk toward the growing General Assembly with them. Some clown had a referee's whistle and was blowing it incessantly, making it echo off the canyons of the capitalistic city. This made it difficult to hear the wisdom proffered by these two Maoists.

"Obama's cool," Chad said. "He's been screwed by the banks too."

"They call his mortgage?" I asked, straight-faced.

"No, but like the banks and Wall Street are against him now. They supported him last time, but now they've turned against him. The whole financial establishment is with Romney."

"Really?" I asked incredulously.

"Oh yeah, they all want Romney cause he's one of them!"

"A banker?" I asked. They ignored me. I was beginning to think these two geniuses were on to me, but then the words I thought I would hear way earlier in our enlightened discourse came from Jacket's mouth as if on perfect cue.

"It all started with Bush!" he said confidently.

"That's what I've heard," I said. "That bastard!"

We walked a little further and they enlightened me some more on the horrors capitalism has foisted upon the world. Everyone who ran a business was scamming to make money and in general the end of mankind as we knew it was in their minds pretty much at hand. And of course it all started with George W. Bush.

As we walked, Rocky and Fenway trotted along contentedly beside us. At one point, Chad bent down and rubbed Rocky's curly head without breaking stride. "Your dogs are pretty chill," he said.

"Thanks," I said.

"In some parts of China they eat dogs," Chad said randomly. He then added, "I could never eat a dog. No way!"

*Probably a vegan*, I thought. I'm sure Rocky must have been relieved.

We got to the end of the block, where the noise and ruckus were now growing louder by the second. "Well, I'd better get on my way," I said. They shook my hand and said goodbye, twice inviting my dogs and I to join them. I politely declined and almost ruined the moment by saying I had to get to work. I turned and began walking back the way I'd come, but paused once to check on the progress of my newfound anarchist friends. I could barely see the top of Chad's pink head as they waded into a sea of fellow patriots determined to save the world from the evil of corporate profits.

More of their ranks were walking toward me, heading to the assembly. First, I assumed it was reinforcements, but then I remembered Jacket saying something about the unions bringing in free sandwiches and bottled water around noon. That explained it! I actually chuckled out loud when a squat woman with a purposeful expression came into view, walking toward the menagerie. She had a stocking cap on her head, a hooded sweatshirt, and a pair of some type of earth shoes from a generation of protests long gone by. In her mittened hands she proudly carried her own hand-painted sign at chest height. In large block letters it proclaimed: "EAT THE RICH!"

*Phew*! I thought. At least it didn't say "EAT THE DOGS."

# CHAPTER FOURTEEN

# MITT, WHAT HAPPENED IN VEGAS?:
*Just When You Thought It Was Safe to Settle on a Frontrunner…*

This past week Muammar Ghadafi was captured and killed in Libya, the President announced our troops would be out of Iraq by the end of the year, and Michele Bachmann's New Hampshire campaign staff abruptly quit (until I heard they'd quit, I didn't even know she had a New Hampshire campaign staff!). The point of this quick headline recap is to point out that much has happened since last Wednesday's GOP presidential debate in Las Vegas. The resulting hangover from that event is still driving the political news cycle and, in many ways, the fate and ongoing fortune of at least at least one participant: Mitt Romney. Like many Republicans, before the GOP Presidential hopefuls took to the stage on the Vegas Strip, I was beginning to believe it was destiny. Pre-ordained. *Fait accompli*. Mitt Romney would be the 2012 GOP nominee. The Republican Party is famous for nominating candidates when it is their turn, and this time it was Mitt's turn. Right? He's a former Governor, and they always make better candidates and better presidents than former legislators. Mitt has money, message, and media, the three M's of modern campaign success. Romney's been racking up endorsements, especially here in New Hampshire and Iowa. Late last week he racked up one of the biggest trophies roaming the Granite State's woods: former NH Governor John H. Sununu, who will serve as a national co-chair of the Romney campaign. It's all been going Mitt's way. He brilliantly avoided the mistake of trying to compete in the deep-fried butter straw poll held in Iowa this summer, leaving that to the all-but-vanquished Michele Bachmann. Then there was the cotillion of Texas Governor Rick Perry, who peaked just a tad early. Herman Cain has begun leading Romney in some early-contest state and national polls, but before last Wednesday you have to admit that we all kind of felt it was a foregone conclusion that Mitt Romney would be the candidate to face Obama. Then came Vegas.

Romney, the guy who has performed steadily and consistently in every debate so far, flopped in Vegas like a bad comic at Caesars Palace. In fact, he came off as a petulant Eagle Scout—interrupting, talking over his opponents, and generally jabbering on like an excitable fourthgrader who'd missed his ADHD medication. It was an embarrassment to watch a smart, savvy politician crumble the first time any real pressure was applied in a debate so far. It was also troubling to think that if the likes of Rick Perry, Ron Paul, Herman Cain, Michelle Bachmann, Rick Santorum, and Newt Gingrich could get under Romney's skin, what in God's name would happen when Romney got on the stage with Barack Obama? Say what you want about Obama, but he's good on his feet and I daresay he would likely look far more presidential than Romney did in Vegas.

Instead of calmly and substantively staving off the collective attacks of Perry and company, Romney somehow convinced himself that by nearly hyperventilating each time someone tried to give him a sharp elbow, he was somehow appearing tough. On the contrary, Mitt was so determined not to allow anyone to land a blow that he consistently talked over a glazed Rick Perry until his opponents wisely let him continue undeterred. That old political adage "never attack your opponent when he's sinking himself" was never more apropos. At one point Perry actually stopped bickering and told Mitt to "have at it" on the issue of which of the two of them was softer on illegal immigration. And so it went.

"It's my turn! It's my turn, it's... it's... it's my turn, Rick. You had your chance. Now it's my chance to speak." Romney chided Perry a number of times, suggesting that the former Texas Governor might be feeling slightly truculent because he had previously suffered a few rough debate performances. That was certainly true. Perry's debate performances have been so lackluster to date, some folks have begun to wonder if he was hypoglycemic! So why did Romney find Perry such a threat that he acted like a nervous schoolgirl when Perry tried to rattle him on the well-known fact that Mitt had hired a couple of Mexican gardeners a few years ago?

This is the oldest story in the anti-Romney attack lexicon, and I cannot imagine how Mitt and his handlers were not more ready for it. The charge first leveled by those fair-minded, non-partisan folks at the *Boston Globe* has already been adjudicated and summarily dismissed. Years back, Romney hired a Massachusetts landscape company, presumably owned and managed by red-blooded Americans, who just happened to hire some illegals. You might think the Governor would have inquired early on if the fellows aerating the lawn at his Belmont home were in fact legal US citizens, but unless they were wearing sombreros during their lunch breaks it might have been a bit insensitive—or at the very least politically incorrect. In hindsight, Mitt should have simply asked, "Que pasa?"

Now, the whole thing has become a cheap political attack metaphor for Romney's alleged "do as I say, not as I do" out-of-touch elitism. Bottom line: Romney's contractor subcontracted illegal aliens. It's not like Mitt smuggled these amigos over the border. Not fair—not even close—and frankly, no thinking person should care. Mitt Romney's position on illegals is quite clear, especially when held up to the sieve of a record the current Governor of Texas has on the issue. So why let Perry get him so hot under the collar? Perry's attempt at a political "gotcha" on a stale and ridiculous charge, now years old, did not require Mitt Romney to laugh like some well-coiffed game show host. He stammered, "Ha-ha-ha-ha Rick… I don't think I've ever hired an illegal in my life, and I am looking forward to finding your facts on that…" It was weird. When Perry tried again, Mitt actually put his hand on the Texas Governor's shoulder and lectured him that if he wanted to be President, he would need learn to let others speak. If Perry's look could kill, Mitt would have been dragged off the stage like an over-matched prizefighter attempting one too many rounds on a Vegas fight night.

At one point in the midst of Romney's whining, he actually begged for help from, of all people, CNN's Anderson Cooper! "Anderson, Anderson, I believe it's… it's my turn. Anderson. Anderson?" The whole thing was unsettling. Don't get me wrong—I like Romney, and frankly believe he would be a strong nominee and a good President. I also believe that among the crop of GOP contenders, Mitt Romney is the GOP's best chance to defeat Obama. But Romney is a better candidate than the guy on stage last week in Sin City. If his advisors think he's looking strong or resolute by talking over the rest of these bit players, they have over-estimated the bit players "big time" (as Dick Cheney once said). The net effect of all of this is that Perry is still the worst single brand intro-duction since New Coke. Mitt Romney and his team should save their slings and arrows for the unlikely event that Perry actually gets himself up off the mat and begins to somehow manage to become relevant in this thing. For now, Herman Cain remains an unlikely strong and relevant force in this race. Mitt Romney? He's still the guy to beat. Let's just hope that what happened in Vegas stays there!

# INTELLECTUALLY, HE'S FINE:
### *But Obama's Brain Isn't Getting the Job Done*

Have you ever noticed that people like to talk about how "smart" our President appears? He is, after all, a Harvard Law school graduate—editor of the *Harvard Law Review*, in fact. Barack Obama is no doubt an articulate fellow. He has a gift for oratory and the ability to comport himself with fine articulation. He can process a reporter's question and respond with a nice bit of prose regarding his position, opinion, and his views on pretty much any issue the President faces both foreign and domestic in a manner that is reassuring at least in terms of his self-expression. Those who attack Obama should not do so assuming he's not bright. No doubt Obama is an intellectual. The problem is, being an intellectual and being effective as President are two very different things.

My liberal friends love to attack George W. Bush, proclaiming portraying him as some ignorant cowboy who managed to mangle the English language while engaging in what they considered "under-intellectualism." Yes, Bush did butcher his langucations (see Chapter 1) from time to time, but to suggest he was stupid is, to use his own word, a "misunderestimation." Bush went to Yale, then Harvard Business School, right? The left snickers that it was Bush family connections that got him into the Ivy League. So how'd Obama get there? I haven't seen an IQ or an SAT score on either of these guys, but the last time I looked, both men have impressive educational dossiers and the appropriate academic credentials to legitimize their intellectual standing. Marginalizing Bush and MENSA-izing Obama is laughable considering the one thing the latter seems to lack entirely: common sense!

You've no doubt heard the old saying that the definition of insanity is doing the same thing over and over and expecting a different result. By his very record and by the policies he has implemented, Obama the "intellectual" has proven that bailouts, failed stimulus, and shovel-ready job boondoggles, mixed with higher taxes and mounting debt simply don't work when it comes to fixing America's broken economy. He's proven that preventing entrepreneurs in a capitalist society from risking their own capital is a death knell to economic recovery. Yet the President persists with the trillion-dollar stimulus, proclaiming that the wealthiest one percent (those individuals, small businesses, partnerships, and LLCs making more than $250,000 a year are somehow calculated in his giant brain as billionaires and millionaires) must "pay their fair share." What the most intellectual of presidents seems to not understand is that without those entrepreneurs who have earned the capital, who do the hiring, who invent the products, and who invest in the development of the future Googles and Apples of the world, America will remain mired in an economic meltdown for generations to come.

I know Warren Buffet thinks he doesn't pay enough in taxes, so perhaps he would consider writing his friend the President a check to get us all out of this mess? For all Obama's brainpower, he is clearly unable to comprehend that most American of economic theories: capitalism creates opportunity. It has for centuries, and it is what has made this country the leading innovator, and center of the economic universe for the last 75 years. Even with his giant brain, Barack Obama cannot comprehend this concept, because it is anathema to him. His life experience as an avowed liberal activist and community organizer keeps him from fundamentally understanding that maybe, just maybe, there might be another way.

But isn't a true intellectual someone who—at least upon occasion—listens and considers that the other side might just have a point? I know the argument from my liberal friends is that the Republicans are just as guilty. They won't give the President a chance, they won't listen, they want to block his agenda at all costs, they're playing politics. Fair enough. But aren't most folks pragmatic enough to look at Obama's policies and realize they have been an abject failure? We're still at over

8% unemployment, our deficit is around 9% of GDP, bankruptcies
are at a record high, and consumer confidence is at an all-time low. In
even the most optimistic polling data, over 70% of Americans view
the country as being on the "wrong track." I'm nowhere near as bright
as Barack Obama, but I can count. It's pretty clear that by almost
any metric standard his policies' effects on this country have been an
abject, complete, and abysmal failure. Now we have riots in the streets.
Those who have proclaimed they are not part of the wealthiest one
percent believe it's time for a little revolution and that Wall Street
and private sector businesses are somehow to blame. Okay, but while
certainly thinking men and women can agree Wall Street has had its
share of bad apples (so too does Washington), let us also agree that
Wall Street has traditionally employed more people than it has screwed
and in fact has created enormous economic opportunity for hardworking Americans who have paid taxes and been by all accounts relatively
productive citizens.

It is absurd that ill-informed "youts" and aging hippies should be
demanding a living wage for NOT working! The fact that the unions
have decided this is good for their own ranks and have joined in the
chorus of misguided malcontents is yet another example of misery using company to get more for itself. One of the reasons America is no
longer leading the world in manufacturing is the arduous and unfair
demands of big labor, whose bloated wages and benefit demands
have made our manufacturing counterparts across the world decide
that they can make the same stuff cheaper and turn a profit while
still managing to employ a lot of people. I'm not suggesting that the
conditions of Chinese labor camps and oppressed societies are something US manufacturers should embrace or emulate, but isn't there
a reasonable way to say to "da union bosses" that consumers are no
longer willing to pay for your unreasonable demands? Americans vote
with their dollars. We can bemoan the Wal-Marts and Japanese car-
makers all we want, but if people don't see the value in what America
builds and sells, they will buy elsewhere—and they are. So why can't
our incredibly smart President accept the plain and simple facts before
him? It simply ain't workin' the way he's thinkin'! You don't have to be
an intellectual to see what is empirically right in front of you. It's not
brains that are the problem here—it's an inability to accept the facts,

plain and simple. America cannot sustain itself under mounting debt and the spend more/tax more gesticulations of Obamian econometrics. Barack Obama is plenty smart alright, but he's leading with his heart and not his ample brain. And I fear his heart is a bleeding one, devoid of any common sense.

# DR. PERRY AND MR. SNIDE:

## *Will the Real Rick Perry Please Commence Campaigning?*

Rick Perry is not a great debater. That may resonate as the political understatement of the year, given the Texas Governor's lackluster performances in the first five GOP cable debates of the 2012 primary season. Given the frequency of these gaggles, it's safe to say Perry has received more exposure than the Juice Man since his steroidal introduction as the GOP challenger to the establishment frontrunner Mitt Romney. It was, however, not to last. Perry's performances in each successive debate made him look like a guy stranded on a JetBlue flight on a snow-covered runway. He was uncomfortable, inarticulate, flat, without energy, and unable to hit applause lines that had clearly been well-rehearsed. Perry again and again performed before a live audience like a novice rather than a man seasoned with 26 years of Texas-style politics.

Then, last weekend in New Hampshire, something inexplicable happened: another Rick Perry showed up for a speech before 400 conservative activists attending a dinner put on by Cornerstone Action.

This Rick Perry was loose, articulate, and in some instances, nearly giddy—laughing at his own jokes, smiling, hamming it up, and definitely playing to the crowd. Perry's lucid performance was so strangely uncharacteristic of the animatronic behavior he has displayed in the campaign so far that some in the room thought he might have been tipsy! A number of media outlets have aired countless cuts of Perry's performance, questioning the Governor's state of mind and his blood alcohol level. That's how totally different the man on stage was. This was not the guy voters in early primary states have seen to date, and it is definitely not the guy Americans have seen so far in televised debate performances.

However, suggesting that the Governor was in some altered state is a bit unfair. Maybe this is the real Perry? Maybe the guy on the stage for those first five debates was a stunt double? Maybe the Rick Perry of debate fame was tired, or his back hurt, or he was on muscle relaxants. Maybe Perry just found his footing (or lost it, depending on your perspective). I was not in the room for the Cornerstone event, but even a neighbor who is a big Perry fan indicated that he was surprised by the Governor's demeanor.

Whichever Rick Perry is the one running for President, he needs to start showing up consistently. The tired, angry, snide Perry appears to not have been anyone's cup of tea based on his plummeting poll numbers in Iowa, New Hampshire, and South Carolina. Maybe the new Rick Perry—the one who showed up the other night in the Granite State—will do better with voters. Lord knows, he couldn't do much worse!

# DEAR HERMAN:

## *An Emergency Memo to Herman Cain*

Emergency Memo
To: Herman Cain
From: Pat Griffin (an admirer from New Hampshire)
Date: 11/2/11
Subject: Please Get Your Story Straight!
CONFIDENTIAL!!

I know it's been a trying last few months. How could you have
known that you would go from pizza mogul to presidential frontrunner in a matter of months? It wasn't supposed to be like this. You
were going to enter the presidential race, raise a little money, and
maybe spend a few bucks of your own—but it would all be earned
back through the book tour. That was the idea. After a meet-and-
greet and signing at the local Barnes & Noble, you do a drop-by for
ninety minutes at some cable debate or maybe and Iowa house party.
Be funny and honest, talk about your business experience, push that
crazy 9-9-9 idea, and every once in a while give Obama a solid poke
from an African-American conservative businessman fed up with
failed liberal economic policies. Remember the whole idea about
playing against type?

So everything's going along pretty well, and all of a sudden you start
getting pretty damn good at this presidential thing. You knock a few
questions out of the park! You answer a moderator's editorialized
question, which made certain assumptions about the 9-9-9 plan,
with a booming "Your assumptions are incorrect!" The crowd loved

it! Of course, you delivered answers with your trademark good humor and passion for doing things differently. Everything was going just fine.

Suddenly your poll numbers started rising and the media herd following you got bigger. You started appearing on "Meet the Press," "This Week," "Face the Nation," and every one of those television gabfests. You were suddenly a rock star! It wasn't your fault. Who knew Rick Perry would fold like a creaky Texas poker table? Who knew that Romney would only garner real support from about a third of GOP voters according to the early polling? Who knew that Bachmann would disappear like some confused Muggle from a Harry Potter installment?

So they started attacking you. That's what they do in politics. First the 9-9-9 plan. They said it wouldn't work. Too simple, wouldn't bring in enough revenue... blah, blah, blah! To your credit, you held your own. When they asked you to name the people who helped you craft the plan, you were pretty crafty about that too. You gave them a name or two, but you also kept 'em guessing as well! The one thing you had going for you was that you were held to a different standard. YOU were NOT a politician! You created jobs, just like Romney! You were a fresh new face with bold ideas, a booming voice, and a million-dollar smile. You were the quintessential American success story! People ate it up! Even after you whiffed the abortion question from that pompous Brit Piers Morgan on CNN, they gave you a pass! You told it like it was, you were honest and straightforward. You didn't have all the foreign policy stuff exactly right, but remember back when then Governor George W. couldn't name the President of Pakistan? No problem.

Then it happened. Someone hit you broadside on the sticky issue of alleged "inappropriate behavior" with a female co-worker from back when you were head of the National Restaurant Association. You denied it, saying it never happened. Then you said it might have happened, but that there had been no settlement with the accuser. Then you said there had been a settlement and that you hoped it hadn't been for much because you didn't do anything. Then you said your mind was becoming clearer. After all, this happened seven years ago! You started to remember that yes, there had been a little problem, and that yes, there was a settlement. But it wasn't really a settlement. It was a severance package given to the accuser, which in your mind is an entirely different kettle of fish. Then you said you only made some comment about her height. How harmless could that be?

Herman, forget the details of what did or did not happen here. The issue is not what you did or said. People in politics have said and done inappropriate things with members of the opposite sex and gone on to do just fine (see Bill Clinton). The problem is, your jive on this matter is starting to make Barack Obama sound like the conductor of the Straight Talk Express! You're not sounding like the Herman Cain who recently became a so interesting. You're sounding like Herman Cain the politician. Not good. Unfortunately, this might be the death knell of what has otherwise been a Cinderella story in the making. When you say one thing one minute and then change your story a short time later, suddenly remembering something that had somehow slipped your mind, you sound like the worst kind of politician. That is, one who's dug himself into an uncomfortable hole and is desperately trying to dig himself out!

Herman, you are better than this. Who's giving you advice? That serial chain-smoking campaign manager of yours in that creepy viral video? If so, what else is he smoking? For what it's worth, here's my advice:

1. Clear this mess up. Tell the truth and be done with it.

2. If your wife knew about this, as you maintain she did, and it was in fact much ado about nothing, then sit down with someone (not Piers Morgan) together and clear this matter up (again, see Clinton: Bill and Hilary)

3. If the woman or women who claim these things are under a sealed confidentiality agreement as part of whatever was settled, you should have the last word on this and let it be. It would be nice if someone from the National Restaurant Association would back you up as well! However those guys too are creatures of Washington with a lot of members and a lot of lobbying to do, so when the phone don't ring it probably will be them.

4. Blame your opponents and the liberal media! Love the witch hunt language. So will conservative money people!

5. Tell that chain-smoking campaign guru of yours to stop making YouTube vids and start running the campaign. Everyone needs to stay on message.

6. Speaking of which: get back on your message. Let people know that they tried to attack your character because they could not compete with your "bold new ideas." Say you've doubled your resolve to stop the vicious negative attacks in politics today and are focusing on making some jobs happen!

7. Put ads up in Iowa and New Hampshire yesterday that turn this mess into a positive. See items one through six for copy points.

8. Do Leno and John Stewart the same night. Give 'em a little of that genuine Cain magic and all this just might disappear faster than you can say "I don't recall." Unless of course there's more to all of this than your letting on. If that's the case, this could be lights out!

Herman, I still love your authenticity and I'm hoping you can get through this one. The best way to start is by doing what comes naturally to you. Be genuine. Be honest. Be Herman Cain!

# HE TOUCHED ME:
## *The Herminator Finally Back on Message?*

It appears Herman Cain may have gotten his mojo back! The GOP contender who has been under fire for alleged sexual harassment while head of the National Restaurant Association seems to have finally gotten his story straight. He has denied the charges, raised over $1.2 million in the last couple of days by blaming what he calls a "witch hunt," and Americans For Herman Cain has posted a strong and effective YouTube video invoking the Clarence Thomas/Anita Hill scandal as a chilling reminder of the ugliness of this whole mess. Today we will find out if the claimant's statement will be released. Let's hope for the sake of decency and consistency that the hospitality industry understands what the term "confidential settlement agreement" really means. Cain's poll numbers continue to show him as the frontrunner for now. If the Herminator plays this thing right it could create a real blowback to those who may have had a hand in promoting this story from the start. The alleged "thin gruel" of this whole mess could have been slowed significantly or even stopped had the Cain campaign been on its "A" game from the start. Cain may end up getting a pass here, but let's hope this serves as a teachable moment. Memo to Mark Block: you are in the big leagues now, dude!

# RICK PERRY STEPS IN IT:
*Debatin's Really Never Been Your Strong Suit!*

Death in politics rarely comes quickly. The end is usually long and slow. It starts with a flub here, a missed opportunity there. One bad debate performance... and then another... and another. Soon the whole world starts to speakin' about you. All your Texas money pals—the oil guys you've been huntin' with for years, the CEOs and bundlers—they start talkin' real quietly around you, not makin' eye contact, slightly afraid they might catch somethin' from you if they linger too close. Then things really start to go downhill. You blow simple debate attack lines on Mitt Romney, the ones those high paid smart guys have helped you with for days! Good lines, "gotcha" lines, the kind you want to show the Republican base you'll use on Obama in the general. But, you whiff. You start the attack just as rehearsed, but like a bad lounge act you somehow mix up the subject with the verb and midway through the line, you get tired and just plain give up like an old coyote, chasing a young prairie rabbit.

Then the liberal media starts sayin' you were never ready for this. Not prepared or disciplined enough to seek the presidency! They start to insinuate that perhaps you're a little lazy, or sleep-deprived, or that your back hurts, or it's the medication—whatever! Then some jerk discovers a rock (that's right, a big ol' Texas rock) that's been sittin' at the entry to some huntin' ranch your daddy grabbed in a land lease a bunch of years ago. Turns out someone painted the "N" word on that rock! That's bad. Real bad! Sure it may have set there for years, but eventually you had one of the farm hands paint over it. After that, you had the damn thing turned on its side so no one would ever see it. What's the big deal?

Couple more debates, one of 'em where you were even sittin'. Now if you're bad at debatin' standin' up, then sure as the sun rises you'll be no good sittin' down! In fact, you were so bad at the Dartmouth College debate you might as well have slept through it and likely woulda done better—at least accordin' to those media libs! Then there was that debate in Vegas, the one where Romney started puttin' his hand on your shoulder like some Southern preacher tryin' to comfort a Texas widow in mournin'. That really steamed you! Speakin' of pastors, there was that creepy pastor Jeffress who introduced you at some Southern convocation of conservative loons, who then went backstage and took it upon himself to tell the media that Romney was the member of a cult! He kept it up, too. Just wouldn't go away. He kept jawin' and jawin' 'bout how old Mitt was a Mormon and Mormons were "cultish." You tried to tell folks that this fella was a man of God and he had the right to his own opinions, and that he wasn't speakin' for Rick Perry. But they wouldn't let up! The polls went further south than a snow goose in winter, and they started diggin' your political grave, right there in front of you. Even though you created all those jobs, and ran Texas—a state bigger than a lot of them half-ass countries in the UN!

You kept showin' 'em the money. You raised a bunch! You put them fancy spots up in Iowa and New Hampshire bout how ol' Rick Perry's "a doer not a talker," but for some reason they just didn't seem to take! Then you gave that crazy speech to the Cornerstone folks up in New Hampshire. All them conservatives all gussied up just to hear you preach some red meat from the book of Perry! You were excited! The room was packed, plus there were a coupla pickup trucks full of media types—all there just for you. You had a hell of a night, and gave a hell of a speech. Problem was, they thought you acted sorta giddy! You giggled, made funny faces, laughed a little too loudly at your own jokes. You even fed 'em that line about how great a state New Hampshire was to have that "Live Free or Die" thing goin' for it. Some folks thought you'd gotten into the moonshine, that maybe your back medicine and a little Texas tea might have caused a bad reaction. But you said you weren't drinkin'! They still wrote about it. You figured those pencil-neck Romney folks put that viral video up usin' all them fancy Star Wars tricks to make it look even worse than it was! Damn that Mitt!

Then, on November ninth, after you'd lingered with the fever of a dyin' campaign, it happened. More than halfway through that stupid debate in Michigan put on by them commies at CNBC you lost your place. You blanked. Had a brain freeze right in the middle of makin' a point to of all people crazy ol' Ron Paul (why you would try to make a point to Ron Paul is a whole 'nother subject). You said it, just like you and the smart guys rehearsed: "It's three agencies of government when I get there that are gone: Commerce, Education and… what's the third one there…?"

Crazy ol' Ron started wavin' his fingers in your face, sayin' "Five," and that got you even more confused. Then smarty-pants Romney jumped in and said "EPA," (like he's tryin' to help!). Damn it all to tarnation if you couldn't for the life of you remember that other federal agency you're intendin' to cut the minute you get two boots on the ground in Washington. And of course that CNBC guy pressed you. "Do you really not know the other department you want to eliminate?"

"Nope. Ah, no, I don't… guess I forgot. Oops!"

It was 54 seconds from the time you opened your mouth to the time you finally shut it after the word "Oops." Seemed like 54 minutes! You knew ol' Herman Cain was off the hook at that point, and you gave Romney another pass, too. You stole the headlines from both of those guys. Now you, Rick Perry, inadvertently created yet another YouTube video to be played millions of times, and this time Romney and the boys didn't even need their fancy editin' equipment. Folks said you had a "brain freeze." They called it your "Stockdale moment," referring to that gadfly Ross Perot's 1992 running mate Admiral James Stockdale, who wandered around the podium and asked, "Who am I and what am I doing here?"

It had been a long, slow, political death. But that was it. That's when they called it. That's when the spin doctors and pundits pulled the sheet over your campaign for the nomination. Put the toe tag on your presidential dreams. Rolled the body to the morgue. Finished, done, over!

Doesn't matter that you tried desperately to save yourself, even walkin' into the spin room with all them varmints from the media. Tellin' 'em, "Glad I wore my boots tonight because I really stepped in it out there!" Problem is, when rigor mortis starts to set in, it doesn't matter how hard the smart guys and spin doctors work. Sure you worked it hard on the talk shows the next day. You did every one of them except Oprah. That thing on Letterman was real cute. But dead's dead.

Rick Perry will not win the Iowa caucus or the New Hampshire primary. He won't win South Carolina or Florida. Most of us knew that before the Michigan debate. In fact, Rick Perry might be in trouble in his native Texas next election, because you know that YouTube video will live on. Somebody somewhere will use it in a commercial or web video to remind everybody in the Lone Star State of the awful, embarrassing night when Governor Rick Perry had that brain freeze. Like they remember Nixon and his sweaty chin against Kennedy and Ed Muskie crying in the snow, folks will remember the night they drove old Perry down.

And everyone who encouraged you to run, the ones who said you can do it, you're ready, you've got money, you created jobs... maybe they should apologize to you for goadin' you into this rodeo in the first place. Maybe they'll actually look you in the eye and say, "Governor, we're sorry. We gave you bad advice, we did you a disservice. You weren't ready for this."

Or maybe they'll just say, "Oops!"

# EYE OF NEWT:
*Gingrich Unexpectedly Back in the
Eye of the 2012 Campaign Storm*

There's something just plain interesting about Newt Gingrich. It's not just that the iconic former House Speaker is smart. He is, I dare say, as smart in terms of his understanding of history, public policy, and political theory as anyone who has ever run for President. By the way, that includes the current occupant of the White House, whom my liberal friends remind me constantly is, in their words, "brilliant" (see Chapter 15). But intellectual capacity can be double-edged sword. If we elected presidents based solely on their IQ, I'm guessing a number of past leaders of the free world simply would not have been chosen by the American electorate. Gingrich is so bright that his intellectualism is actually a bit of a stumbling block for him. Newt sees things the rest of us simply can't. And when we can't, he gets a little grumpy with us. His frustration and complete disdain for the liberal main stream media is a big hit with conservatives. Anyone who can look PBS's Charlie Rose squarely in the eye and ask "You're kidding me, right?" with a straight face in response to a ridiculously left leaning and totally biased question will get and deserves supportive howls from a GOP audience. To Maria Bartiromo on last week's CNBC cable scrum in Michigan: "You want me to tell you how I would fix the healthcare system in 30 seconds?" More howls and cheers from the faithful.

Gingrich has made a pretty good political living defying convention and conspiring against the mainstream media. He regularly earns cheap applause lines from the conservative masses, and it makes him stand out from the crowd. The Speaker is always ready to remind everyone in the room—including the self-important scribes from the left-leaning media—that these endless cable debates are (in his mind) silly. They are an exercise in intellectual dishonesty, and not substantive because of the bias of the questions and the questioners. He reminds us that the formats are also ridiculous: lighting rounds, candidates questioning each other, one-word answers—"A simple yes or no, please." Sometimes these things with their buzzers and bells indicating time is up remind us of a JV round of Jeopardy instead of an honest to goodness contest of ideas and policy.

These game-show "gotcha" formats are set up to make the candidates trip up, look stupid, and entertain the rest of us with a circus-style political food fight. The Speaker will have no part of it. While he has offered only some criticism of his fellow Republicans to date, Gingrich smartly spends most of his time on President Obama. Even better, he gets the joke: a good number of media types are trying to make Republicans look bad so a flailing Obama will look better. Gingrich reminds us again and again what he did with the contract with America and what he and Ronald Reagan did or tried to do in terms of taxes cutting taxes and spending. I, for one, love it! If the Speaker would agree to teach a course on political science, philosophy, or history on ANY university campus, students of all political persuasions would flock to his class. He has taught at the college level before. Between numerous books and movies, endless media appearances and speeches, Gingrich has offered his take on a number of topics to all who would listen. This makes him more interesting and far more informed than anyone else seeking the presidency.

The real problem for Newt is that his intellectual heft is both a gift and a burden. You've heard the old line about asking someone to turn on a light, and then they proceed to give you a lesson on electricity? That's Newt. He is so smart, so burdened by his intellectual cargo, his understanding of the historic root cause of everything that has occurred in this world since creation, that he is hard-pressed to give simple, easily digestible debate answers and brief sound bites. It's sometimes hard to listen to Newt Gingrich because the answers are rarely simple, and they are often too complicated for most of mortals to fully comprehend. One also gets the distinct feeling that Newt's frustration in having to explain why fundamental non-Keynesian economic theory is fatally flawed makes him feel a bit put out! Gingrich is far from a perfect man, and he admits it, personally and politically. He also understands that his inability to kiss babies and dumb down the complex issues facing the next President is his Achilles heel in this race. "Too smart to be able to have patience enough to enlighten the rest of us" is how one reporter recently put it. True enough.

But in the last week, the Newt boomlet has put him back in contention, and he is beginning to rise in the polls like a Phoenix after his disastrous presidential campaign first began. There was a lack of discipline. A disinterest in the process of the campaign. An unwillingness to follow convention, and an unfortunate willingness to go on vacation (Hawaii and the Greek Islands earlier this year), which made his supporters, staffers, former staffers, and the press question his real conviction and commitment to conducting a serious campaign. The good news for Newt is that he is an established political brand, and we Republicans like established brands. His basic personal and political problems are already public, and I believe they are very much baked into his political brand. Republicans know Newt. While he ain't perfect, they pretty much know where he stands and what he stands for, and he stands in stark contrast to the President.

So as the Newt boomlet begins, watch him carefully. He is savant-like in his explanation of why he believes what he believes. Whether you agree with the guy politically or not, you know his positions and know that he is unafraid. The refreshing part of Gingrich is his ability to grasp and respond to complexities and allow voters to understand why he believes what he does. While he can occasionally lapse into the world of policy wonkdom (which may make some voters' eyes glaze over on more complex global political issues), the Speaker often demonstrates the uncanny ability to take complex issues and distill them down to key historic and policy points. This makes these things simple and easy to understand in straightforward, unequivocal terms. Try listening to Barack Obama attempt to candidly and precisely explain his position on a complex and dicey political issue. He can't! I must admit, there is a part of me that would love to see those untimed Lincoln-Douglas style debates between Gingrich and Obama. Two smart guys, no over-styled media questioners with a buzzer after 30 seconds, and the artful and articulate conversation of two men who are informed and fully prepared to take their very different ideologies and views of the world to the voters.

Gingrich now finds himself being taken seriously, finally, as a conservative alternative to the increasingly unstoppable Mitt Romney. With it will come yet another opportunity to connect with voters, provided the Speaker takes one important lesson from his political hero Ronald Reagan: be patient and pleasant. Smile and bring some sunny optimism into what is an otherwise very frightening time in this world. Offer the voters a chance to fix this mess. Communicate gently, bring it down to the level of the rest of us mere mortals, and maybe, just maybe we will understand. Newt Gingrich has a shot to stage a political comeback, to earn a new relevance in the GOP race, but only if he can deal with the uninformed masses he appears to disdain. As his poll numbers rise, he will be pulled into the eye of the political storm. If nothing else, we will be seeing and hearing a lot more from the political enigma that is Newt Gingrich. For better or worse, he is back in contention and back in the eye of the political storm. The real question is, how long can he last?

# THEY SHOOT HORSE THIEVES, DON'T THEY?:
*Perry's New Big Idea Is Ripped Off and Wrong!*

At a speech yesterday in Iowa, embattled Rick Perry desperately tried to make his campaign relevant. The last time a guy from Texas had been through the kind of beating it took place at The Alamo! Perry launched the brilliant idea of revising government so that members of Congress would spend less time in Washington and more time with their constituents. "Send 'em home!" was Perry's cheap applause line.

Wow, a brilliant "reinventing government" idea from a guy who has been in politics for 26 years! Perry's refrain is no doubt an attempt to distance himself from the other "politicians" in the GOP field—especially those who have spent considerable time in Washington. (Newt, he's talking to you!) The idea of taking advantage of the low approval ratings for Congress must have sounded really innovative to the imagineers back in Perry's policy shop in Texas. They surely must have seen it as a "bold new idea," as Herman Cain would say. It's plenty bold. The idea of keeping members of Congress out of Washington so they can spend less and not hurt us more is a compelling Republican call (especially when the Democrats controlled Congress). Memo to Rick Perry: you're running for the Republican nomination for President. Maybe you haven't noticed it lately, but Republicans control the Congress! Not only that, but Perry's "send 'em home" rhetoric is also cut-and-pasted from the 1996 presidential campaign of former Tennessee Governor and current U.S. Senator Lamar Alexander, who spoke of the ineffectiveness of the Democratic Congress by imploring: "Cut their pay and send them home!" From a purely political standpoint the words rang much truer then than they do now.

One more attempt to make someone—anyone—pay attention to Perry's campaign, which appears to have little left to say! I'm sure members of the Republican majority in Congress who have been trying to fight President Obama's healthcare reform bill ("Obama-Care"), fighting against more stimulus spending boondoggles, would argue that they have been plenty busy trying to protect the rest of us from the ridiculous policies of the left. Why, then, in the middle of the battle does Perry want to call for retreat? This is political reality, not The Alamo! When Lamar Alexander came up with this clarion call originally, it was because the Democrats were spending money like drunken sailors and had been for more than 30 years! It was time for a populist Republican to call for a revolutionary change to get these people away from literally legislating (and taxing) the country to death. The line worked when Senator Alexander used it in his presidential campaign, and he came closer than anyone thought to an upset victory in New Hampshire. It should be noted that Perry has absolutely no chance of doing the same.

Maybe he should look for better writers, or at least to recent history, before he pirates lines from previous campaigns—especially when those lines whack members of his own party. The last guy I remember who plagiarized lines from other politicians was Joe Biden. During his presidential run in 1987, he ripped off the speeches of former British Labor leader Neil Kinnock. At least Biden made it to being Vice President. Rick Perry won't even get that far!

# CHAPTER TWENTY-TWO

# STORM CLOUDS ON THE HORIZON FOR MITT:
## *The Race for the GOP Nomination is On!*

No one should be surprised. We all knew this would happen. We just didn't expect the cast of characters to be who they are. Mitt Romney, long the frontrunner and the winner (almost by default) of nearly every presidential TV debate scrum since last June, has a couple of real challengers in early nominating contests in Iowa and New Hampshire. They are Newt Gingrich (whose political star was already beginning to surge when he received the coveted endorsement of the New Hampshire *Union Leader* newspaper) and quadrennial candidate Texas Congressman Ron Paul. While Paul will never be the GOP nominee (much less the President), he will receive enough votes in Iowa and New Hampshire to likely hurt Romney and help Gingrich. His campaign—the otherworldly imaginarium of Dr. Paul—is a strange and interesting enterprise comprised largely of a devoted group of conservative-minded libertarians who favor legalizing pot and returning to the gold standard. Paul's anti-war, anti-government, pro-"smoke it if you have it" brand of politics make for interesting political theatre, even though his chances of success are nil. However strange it may be, the same Dr. Paul will likely be what Marlon Brando called "a contenda" at least in early contests, mainly because his fan base is revved up. They don't have much else to do, so they will turn out for him on primary day. What's more, Paul's impact on the New Hampshire race will likely be in the 12 to 15 percent range, if not a tad higher! That's a hunk of conservative and independent votes sucked out of the field and unavailable for others to fight over. Add to this Herman Cain's sudden "reassessment" of his campaign (read: "He's cooked"), and conservatives in Iowa and conservatives and independents in New Hampshire are left with only one viable choice: Gingrich.

With Cain out, what's left of his conservative base may coalesce behind the former speaker. Without a surprise first, second or third-place win for Bachmann or Santorum in Iowa, they are out of gas and will likely not even make it to the "Live Free or Die" state. Their supporters also go elsewhere—likely Gingrich. Many conservatives have never liked or trusted Mitt Romney, and my bet is that the *Union Leader* will regularly remind voters in New Hampshire about the "evolution" of Romney's political positions. What's more, they will contrast Gingrich against Romney and President Obama together. That's right, the ultimate insult: Romney is Obama with a better track record playing the markets. That may not be fair, but Americans are angry with Obama's failures and his broken promises, and the case will be made that replacing Obama with Romney will be akin to "tinkering at the margins." If voters want real change and the chance to see strikingly different views of America, the economy, and our country's place in the world, then an Obama/Gingrich contest may be just the answer. While many in the Republican establishment are concerned about Newt's electability in a national campaign, Romney's inevitability argument has begun to slip away with new polls that show Gingrich even or, in some cases, significantly ahead at least for now. This could all change and likely will, but it ain't over yet.

That means Romney is left in the unenviable position of holding his weakening frontrunner status (at a high in New Hampshire last week in the low 40s) from now until the primary on January 10th. This is a near-impossible task, as voters know the former Massachusetts Governor well and at least 60% are currently against him. I learned the hard way back in the 1992 campaign as an advisor to President George H. W. Bush (then the incumbent President), and in 2000 with another Bush, that the imperial campaigns of pre-ordained frontrunners are subject to the simple laws of gravity. Romney may be the best-known, but what goes up must come down. Gravity is not working in Mitt's favor. In fact, with nearly every conceivable endorsement in his quiver, Romney may have peaked a bit too early. More frustrated voters are starting to pay attention and are looking for something else. Even if Mitt pulls off early wins in Iowa and New Hampshire, will it be enough to satisfy southern conservatives who will be waiting in South Carolina and Florida like hungry wolves if they have a more ideologically conservative choice?

Then there's the Iowa question. Is Romney playing there? Is there in fact an "underground campaign?" Will Romney attack Gingrich as he went after John McCain in 2008? My recollection is that that didn't work out so well. Iowa is a place where the Republican electorate is stratospherically more socially conservative than New Hampshire, but still a contest where the press will hold the frontrunner to a high standard. The inability to win Iowa or even make it a close contest could hurt Romney even more, and create for Gingrich not just a campaign opening, but a movement. Movements in politics are dangerous things if you're the perceived frontrunner and the movement ain't behind you!

The press will already hold Romney to an exceptionally high (and unreasonable) standard of exactly what will constitute a win in New Hampshire. For that reason, all Gingrich would need to do is make it close here for a moral victory, which the press would love as the campaign heads to South Carolina.

What about Jon Huntsman? He's a good, reasonable guy, and the press can't understand why New Hampshire hasn't fallen for him, but the fact is it just hasn't and likely won't. I see Huntsman finishing fourth behind Ron Paul in New Hampshire—the only place he's running. That's lights out! For now, at least, Mitt and Newt will duke it out for the title. As for Rick Perry? There could be yet another act for the Texas Governor, but probably not. If Perry begins even a modest surge it would be the greatest comeback since Lazarus! Probably not gonna happen. And what of Rick Santorum, the working class swing state senator who claims he will have visited all 99 counties in Iowa by the time the caucus balloting takes place? Iowa likes grass roots politics and the one thing Santorum will be able to claim: he is the poster child for retail. It would be a huge surprise that a guy who has languished in the polls for almost a year suddenly showed up, but stranger things have happened.

So it begins. The field winnows, candidates are eliminated by too much scandal or not enough oxygen. In many cases, they will be eliminated by voters who wish to make their votes a protest of the status quo, not an endorsement for a slightly different version. The race that many assumed would not even be a contest is now officially up for grabs, and there are still five weeks until the Iowa caucuses. The TV has started, the endorsements have begun, and the race for the GOP nomination is looking like the most interesting one in a very long time. Presidential campaigns in New Hampshire are a lot like the weather here. As Mark Twain once said, "If you don't like it, just wait a few minutes." Looks to me a like there's a storm front coming in, and it could get very nasty and maybe—just maybe—get close!

# DEAR MR. PRESIDENT (PART 1):

*A (Possible) Secret Memorandum to President Obama from Chief Political Guru David Axelrod (a Little Good News!)*

With the primary season in full swing, I've wondered what communication might look like between the Guru and his boss in the White House. I suspect it might look a little something like this:

Memorandum
CONFIDENTIAL
To: POTUS
From: David Axelrod
Subject: An Update on the GOP Field
Date: Dec. 5, 2011

I'm happy to report some good news for a change, which might make you feel a little better this week about your prospects for reelection in 2012 than you have the last few months. I know I told the folks in New Hampshire when last I visited in the fall that your prospects to retain the White House in 2012 would be a "Titanic Struggle." My bad on that one sir, but things may be looking up!

First: finally a little brightness on the domestic economic front. Last week, the unemployment rate in the US dropped to 8.6%, the lowest level since right after you took office. Stocks rallied on Wall Street above the 12,000 mark on news that the Fed is somehow going to stabilize overseas markets. How they expect to do it is beyond me, but what the hell, voters seem to be buying it! On the consumer confidence side, retailers report that Black Friday, that big shopping day after Thanksgiving, was pretty darn good. So good, in fact, that shoppers were lined up days before the sales, camping out in mall parking lots and forming lines like they were waiting for Justin Bieber concert tickets! So good that some nutcase in Los Angeles reportedly pepper-sprayed her fellow shoppers who threatened to get in the way of her buying the new X-Box! Now that's the kind of consumer confidence only a true leader like you can inspire! I suggest we take full credit for all of this. Perhaps we can ask the ad guys to come up with something for the web that suggests your policies have brought the Occupy Wall Street loons' anarchy out of our city parks and right into the aisles of Best Buy! Do you think Mitt Romney could do that? No way!

Regarding Mitt: you might find this unbelievable, but while you were traveling on the Asian Peninsula, shopping with the girls in DC, and pardoning that Thanksgiving turkey, some really strange stuff has been happening in the Republican presidential scrum. Mitt's in big trouble! That's good news. Let's face it, Romney may have his problems. But in a general election the whole "outside Washington, created jobs in the private sector, successful businessman" thing might be a real problem for us. Not to worry! Romney's polling numbers are dropping like Norwegian Spruce trees this time of year! He's been the frontrunner since the beginning, but in Iowa, New Hampshire, South Carolina, and even Florida he's losing ground faster than you can say "community organizer!" Romney can't seem to catch a break! The Tea Party doesn't trust him, independents see him as too "establishment" and timid, and the rest of the GOP seems to view him as an elitist out-of-touch insider who happens to be the poster child for the one percent. The others have made him a serial flip-flopper, which is good for us, because (as you know) we have a penchant for promising the world and delivering not much!

Another thing about Mitt: he's finally doing some television interviews. He did one with Brett Baier from Fox News last week and stammered and stumbled through the thing, getting all prickly when Baier threw a few softballs at him on alleged changes in his positions. Romney was awful, and apparently complained after the interview that Baier was unfair and unnecessarily rough on him. If he thinks Fox is tough, wait until our comrades over at MSNBC and the network polit-news bureaus get done with him! Romney still has money and a ground game in New Hampshire, but he seems to be spending less time in Iowa than a guy running for mayor of Brooklyn! Those corn-fed conservatives apparently spook Mitt a bit, but he has started running some TV ads there (like five a week). The ad buy is a little light, but he has officially decided to play in the Hawkeye State. The media will hold him to a standard that is nothing short of first place there. His main rival for now (and you're not going to believe this) is Newt Gingrich!

Yep. Newt! He's beating Romney in almost every poll in early primary states. The same Newt Gingrich that had that ethics problem a few years back and wound up leaving the speakership in, let's just say, a bit of a cloud. The same Newt who's been a creature of Washington for the last 45 years has suddenly become the GOP's populist outsider! The same Newt Gingrich, thrice-married and divorced, and who lobbied—excuse me, "provided history lessons"—for a big fee to Freddie and Fannie just before the housing bubble burst! The same Newt who owed all that money to Tiffany's and who took off for the Greek Islands and Hawaii in the middle of the campaign!

Sir, this may sound too good to be true, but it is! What's more, just as Newt's rising in the polls, he gets endorsed by the *Union Leader* newspaper in New Hampshire! Sure, it helps him with conservatives in the Granite State, but more importantly those *Union Leader* boys have been on every program except "Ellen" so far touting the reasons they are for Newt and not for Mitt! Publisher Joe McQuaid (you remember him, right?) was even on "Meet the Press" yesterday! This endorsement makes Newt legit from Des Moines to Delray Beach, and I get the feeling the *UL* will start the anti-Mitt stuff real soon. Here's the really good news: Newt Gingrich is still smart, but he works (unlike Romney) without a net! No teleprompter, no talking points, no script! Can you imagine? Newt Gingrich still seems to say whatever is on his mind!

This is great. As you know, we focus group everything, including your choice of neckties, and he's bound to screw up sooner or later! Bottom line, Gingrich is mounting a real challenge for Romney, and should Mitt decide to fully engage in Iowa and New Hampshire with the negative stuff, there could be some real blowback! Remember what happened to Mitt in 2007 when he went after John McCain? Not pretty!

Oh, a couple of other things, sir: Herman Cain turns out to allegedly be a serial adulterer. Not just one or two. There's more! Including a woman named Ginger who may have been an adult dancer (at least we think that based on her name) she alleges the Herminator carried on a 13-year affair with her! She's a little fuzzy on some of the details and she looks like a stunt double for Stiffler's Mom in those American Pie movies, but everyone's all over this thing and Cain now makes Bill Clinton look like a Boy Scout! Cain's done, so where does his support go? To Newt of course! Score a few more points for the Speaker. I'll tell you this: Whatever is left of Cain's supporters who have not yet abandoned ship, they sure ain't going to Romney-ville!

Then there's Ron Paul. One thing I know for sure is that he has the alien vote sewn up! They will definitely turn out in these early primaries. Sure, Paul's a little nuts, but he's been to the mother ship, he knows all the conspiracy theories, and he's convinced that the whole Area 51 thing is real (he may even have seen the photos). In any event, Paul voters are coming out for him in Iowa and New Hampshire, which means if nothing else he will be a pain in Romney's ass as well. I see him with 12 to 17 percent of the vote in New Hampshire. That's a chunk of primary voters, all of whom believe that *Close Encounters of the Third Kind* was a History Channel documentary!

Jon Huntsman is still camped out in New Hampshire, and in some polls he's barely gaining low double digits. Assume Huntsman's good for 10 to 12 percent, but not much more. Assume Bachmann and Santorum each get a couple of points, maybe 5 to 9 percent between them, and the math becomes even tougher for Mitt. Gingrich will likely win over more partisan and angry independent voters. He'll win with a plurality of the roughly 55% of the vote left when you factor out the other candidates. So there you have it, sir. We've barely started to gear up and it's looking like the GOP may serve us up Newt Gingrich on a platter just in time for Christmas!

Some are saying that Newt will be tough in the general election, particularly when it comes to debates. That could be, but sir, think of all the stuff we have on the guy! Our Oppo Research Team of 600 socialist interns in the White House basement have been hard at work, and we think we can make Newt look more evil than we made McCain look by at least a couple of football fields! Relax during the holidays, sir, things are going just fine. The likelihood of Mitt waking from his primary slump and slumber is looking slim. Let's hope the Romney guys stay asleep, because Newt could become the GOP's worst nightmare. If he isn't now, rest assured we will make him exactly that! Keep up the good work, sir. Whatever you do, don't do much of anything right now. The GOP appears to be doing it for us!

★

# CHAPTER TWENTY-FOUR

# GENTLEMEN, HAVE A SEAT:
### *The Lincoln/Douglas Debate: Rare and Well Done.*

Here's the gist of a conversation I heard recently over dinner at one of New York's truly great steak houses:

Waiter: "We're known here for both our wet and dry-aged 100% Wagyu beef. The chef recommends it rare to medium rare."

Diner: "I'll have that, but I like mine well done, not just singed or sushi-like. I want it cooked through and through. Take all the excitement out of it. Put it on the fire and let it sit there a good long time and sizzle!"

Waiter: "But sir, the chef fears that a well-done preparation could result in a flavorless, dry steak."

Diner: "Thanks, but I'd like it well done."

Waiter: "Yes, sir."

Twenty minutes later, the same waiter delivers the dinner entrees to the table. Upon presentation, the fellow quoted above pokes a fork at his steak and says, "This steak is dry!"

Waiter: "I told you, sir, dry is… well, dry. You insisted."

Diner: "I just took a bite and it's dry and has no flavor! Bring me another steak and this time I'll have it rare!"

I recap this scene because ordering a steak is a lot like ordering presidential candidates to tell us what they really think, take their time, and not speak in sound bites or quips. We the voters argue we would get a clearer and more thoughtful impression of candidates and their positions on important issues by eliminating "gotcha questions" from journalists, lightning rounds, bells, whistles, horns, and the chance to win a new car from the standard format televised debates. Everyone, including the candidates, hate the 30 second rebuttal to the 60 second answer. The whole debate thing has become a bit of a joke. Splashy sets, live tweets, e-mail questions, and real voters live via video link from some county far away from the actual debate venue that it's barley in the same time zone. It's all Hollywood, all sizzle, not even much steak and not well done. Remember however, when it comes to well done, you have to be careful what you wish for. Well done is safe, not sexy. Well done takes longer to cook. It's not quick. Like our friend at the steak house learned, well done can be flavorless and a tad dry.

On Monday I was fortunate enough to moderate a Lincoln/Douglas-style debate between Governor Jon Huntsman and Speaker Newt Gingrich, presented by The New Hampshire Institute of Politics at St. Anselm College in Manchester, NH. The debate was put together jointly and cooperatively by the Huntsman and Gingrich campaigns. They agreed to discuss the increasingly important issues of foreign policy and national security using ten pre-agreed topics, ranging from immigration to the Middle East and from Asia and the Pacific Rim to the War on Terror. The candidates were completely unfettered and pretty much uninterrupted by any game show silliness or food fights. For 90 minutes, two of the most thoughtful candidates in the GOP field agreed to sit next to each other at a simple wooden table and speak at length on each topic. This promised to be different, and it was. But a number of people who attended the event, including some in the national press corps, thought that all this serious stuff sounded well and good, but it wasn't great TV. It was, as one reporter wrote, " It was so dry you could blow the dust off it."

The point is this: for anyone seriously concerned about the state of our world, from domestic and economic challenges to what precise threat an Iran with nuclear capabilities might pose, then this kind of dry is very important.

Both Gingrich and Huntsman proved incredibly knowledgeable, and spoke in great detail on the complexities, challenges, and real threats the next President of the United States will face in the international arena. We elect presidents for a whole lot of reasons, but if we would like a substantive one—especially on foreign policy—I respectfully suggest you find the re-broadcast (or search for the discussion on You-Tube). This is a dry ninety minutes, but it's a complete college semester's worth of content that every voter should see and hear. The fact is that both of these candidates—one the current frontrunner, the other a man who has literally staked his entire campaign on being heard and exposed to the voters of New Hampshire—are both impressive. Either would make most Americans sleep better at night than the all-too-"rare" Barack Obama, who himself is a lot more sizzle than steak when dealing with the complexities and very real dangers America faces across the world. I'll take my President dry, thank you!

★

# CHAPTER TWENTY-FIVE

# RON PAUL:

*Is Everyone's Crazy Uncle Headed for a Victory Lap in Iowa?*

It's pretty clear how things are trending in the Hawkeye State right now. More and more political pundits are agreeing that Ron Paul might actually win Iowa, with Newt Gingrich coming in second. Crazier things have happened... but not much crazier! The good news: there's still time for this to change-but not much. The real news here is that Paul or Gingrich winning Iowa could relegate Mitt Romney to a third or even fourth-place finish here, depending of course on how well Rick Perry's prosecution of the battle against Obama's "war against religion" turns out. The Bachmann, Perry, and Santorum stuff sells well with religious conservatives in Iowa. Perry is spending a boatload on TV, Bachmann is the local favorite (born in Waterloo, Iowa), and Santorum is the only candidate in the GOP field so far to have visited all 99 Iowa counties! (The guy should at least get a tote bag for that!)

The good Dr. Paul may be warming up to steal the Iowa caucuses. Based on his organization and die-hard supporters, you can be sure the Paul folks will turn out on caucus night. Since they'll be armed with emergency drinking water, first-aid kits, tire chains, and organic energy bars, I respectfully suggest that no precinct captain in his right mind try to get between a group of Paul supporters and the entryway door of any caucus site. Paul's supporters will show up early and stay until the 46th ballot at three in the morning for their guy if that's what it takes.

Mitt Romney's got to be hoping for just such a possibility. Ron Paul is the best thing he can hope for to help slow the momentum of Newt Gingrich. The problem for Romney is that New Hampshire is suddenly becoming slippery ground for him, as polls tighten and Newt continues to surge. If Mitt loses Iowa, then loses New Hampshire (and by lose I mean he doesn't win it significantly enough in the eyes of the national media to be a clear victory), he heads toward some rough sledding. First in South Carolina (where Gingrich holds double-digit leads in most polling) and then on to Florida, a far more conservative primary event than most people realize. Mitt could go 0 for 4 in the early contests. Now, Team Romney has lots of resources and plenty of cash still on hand. They claimed this week that they are prepared for a long nominating contest. But let's face it: until the last couple of weeks they couldn't begin to imagine the Newt-mare scenario unfolding before their eyes today. Something tells me if Paul wins Iowa, Newt wins New Hampshire. Then we proceed with a very long and messy GOP nominating process.

Just twenty more days until the caucus. For those of you who can't wait for the Fed to be history, get your gold bars shined up! You may just have a whole week between Iowa and New Hampshire to fantasize that your guy Ron Paul could somehow become President! Make a lot of noise, raise hell in New Hampshire, order reinforcements from the planet Kobar, and smoke 'em if you got 'em (be careful with that, though, because for now at least it's still illegal here). Your guy Ron Paul might just march into the Granite State as the victor of the Iowa Caucus, and that would be amazing! Imagine 500 college kids, all trained at hempfests across the nation, marching on the State House, or greeting a victorious Dr. Paul as he arrives at Manchester Airport in the wee hours of the post-caucus morning with a full kazoo symphony of "Hail to the Chief"! It would certainly make for the start of a very interesting week! A whole lot more interesting than the week Mitt Romney might have in store for him. Party on, Ron!

★

# CHAPTER TWENTY-SIX

# COOKING WITH NUTS:
## *The Ron Paul Family Cookbook*

I opened the mail late last night and noticed that there was a hefty envelope addressed to my wife. The return address was that of the Paul Family of 845 Plantation Drive in Clute, Texas. Hmm…. I opened the envelope. What to my wondering eyes should appear but a complimentary full-color copy of the *Ron Paul Family Cookbook*! Well, you can imagine how pleased I was. My wife is a great cook who is always looking for new things to whip up for our own family soirées. I took the liberty of thumbing through the thing just to see exactly what it was Mrs. Paul fancied in the way of down home Texas cookin'. I was a little surprised not to find fish sticks, as I assumed that was what she was best known for. I found Fay's Pot Pie (of the chicken variety), Banana NUT Bread (not surprising), Impossible Pie, The Razzle Bo-Dazzle Pork Tenderloin, and Mom's Hot Slaw just to name a few. One recipe I think it's safe to assume the Griffin's won't be trying is Mrs. Paul's Cherry-Pineapple Dump Cake. Let's just say it didn't sound quite as appetizing as some of the rest of the dishes.

Sprinkled among the various recipes are snapshots of the Paul family, including son Rand being sworn into the U.S. Senate while standing next to a slightly uncomfortable Vice President Joe Biden in the old Senate Chamber. I was also pleased to see enclosed a personal letter (well, not quite personal, but made to look like Mrs. Paul handwrote it) with the heading "From the Desk of Carol Paul." The note not only introduced the lovely cookbook, but also took the time to introduce us to her husband in a bit more depth. It was actually a very nice letter, and I for one appreciated Mrs. Paul taking all that time out of the kitchen to write to us. By the way, the cookbook also features another little extra on the back pages just after the recipe for Creole Praline Yam Casserole. It's titled "The American Dream, Through the Eyes of Mrs. Ron Paul," which she informally signs: "Carol."

I was thinking about this idea. If the presidential thing somehow doesn't work out for the congressman, and Mrs. Paul has to keep cooking for her brood down in Clute without the assistance of the White House chef, I'm thinking I've got a great pitch for the Food Network for a new show! How about *Cooking Like Crazy with The Pauls*? Forget *Iron Chef*. How about *Gold Standard Chef*? The Pauls could make a fortune! That would mean more cookbooks, personal appearances, and the potential to push Paula Deen and the Barefoot Contessa right off the network! I noticed the Pauls do have a lot of recipes that feature nuts. How about *Cooking with Nuts*, or maybe *Down Home with the Pauls*. Forget the Neeleys!

If this works, there could be a whole line of cooking utensils as well. Cut the Government Waste Cutlery, or the famous Federal Government Chopping Board. I know it's all a little far-fetched, but you have to admit it's great marketing! It's also a great way to market the Ron Paul presidential campaign. You don't actually think Ann Romney or Callista Gingrich are going to send you a cookbook, do you? This is good ol' fashioned politicking in a down-home neighborly way. Dr. and Mrs. Paul clearly know that the way to a voter's heart is through his or her stomach!

One last thing. There was a little contribution card in the envelope with a place for like-minded folks who appreciate the cookbook and who might like to "Help elect Ron as our next President." Well, I must tell you, Mrs. Paul had me at the Mom's Hot Slaw, so I decided ol' Ron could count on me. I sent 25 bucks. Sorry, Congressman, I had to send cash. I was fresh out of 25-dollar gold bars. Just get it to the bank fast before the Feds go and lose it somewhere.

Now, I'm not supporting Ron Paul. In fact, regular readers know I am not supporting any candidate this election except for the one I vote for on January 10th. But I do like Mrs. Paul, and I appreciate the thoughtful cookbook and her nice words. She seems like a lovely woman, and I need to get on her good side. If this Food Network thing works out, I'm hoping to get a cut of the empire. After all, it was my idea!

*Ron Appetit*!

# IOWA:
## *So Cold You Can Feel the Heat!*

There's a change in the presidential air in Iowa.

Last Thursday, the cold wind that blows through the plains of the Hawkeye State finally carried the bone-chilling hallmark of a true Iowa winter. All things considered, it's been mild for this time of year. That is, outside of the political universe, where things have been getting white-hot. Maybe that's why snow hasn't accumulated much on the ground in Des Moines or Polk County. Call it the political global warming of Iowa, the El Nino of the plains, The Santa Anna Winds of Sioux City. All the heated political rhetoric that has spilled out of the legion halls, churches, and town meetings has made the temperatures downright balmy across Iowa's fruited plains. Thursday changed all that.

Suddenly the weight of being Newt Gingrich was starting to feel unbearable. The tonnage of negative TV from the pro-Mitt Romney Super PAC, the anti-Newt ads from the Ron Paul wing nuts going right for the jugular, the negative mail stuffed in Iowa mailboxes with such volume that Christmas cards could be delayed until well after the Yuletide: all of this is, to say the least, taking a toll. The Newt Boom that made the former Speaker the official frontrunner in Iowa, South Carolina, and Florida seems to be leveling off. It may even be ticking back more than anyone realizes. Strange things are blowing with the now-chilly Iowa winds. Republican conservatives are taking yet another look, re-assessing the field one last time and trying to determine just who they might put up to defeat Lord Obama once and for all. Part of the electorate longs to see Gingrich take to the debate stage with the President, and in typical Newt fashion teach him a thing or two about free markets, reducing the size and scope of government, and the dangers of apologizing for America from one third-world country to another. Yes, that would be interesting all right.

But is the spectacle of a debate as compelling as a win for the GOP? In recent weeks this has become less about defeating Obama and more about teaching Mitt Romney that he wasn't principled or consistently conservative enough for the 30% of Iowa Republicans who define themselves as "conservative." But with the sudden chill in the Iowa air a new realization is dawning (in no small part because others have spent a fortune putting the negative hit on Newt). While Gingrich is compelling in so many ways, he may not be the right guy right now to be the GOP standard-bearer. The "baggage" charge is gaining support: all that money from Freddie Mac, Newt's temperament and his leaving Congress (as one ad puts it, "in disgrace") due to ethics violations. You know what they say about throwing enough "you know what" against the wall. Eventually some of it sticks. Based on Newt's most recent Iowa polling, some of it has.

Now we find ourselves in what appears to be a three-way contest for the heart and soul of Iowa. It's Newt, Paul, and back from the dead: one Mitt Romney! My suspicion and prediction is that Ron Paul's organization of battle-tested wingnuts might still be enough to allow the good doctor to pull off a win—unlikely, but possible. In that case, say good-bye to any legitimacy given to the good sense and judgment of Iowa voters. They gave us Michele "I don't hate Muslims" Bachmann in this summer's Iowa Straw Poll. If they do in fact give Paul a victory, we can assume that that the extreme right wing (of the right wing) has hijacked both the sensibility and the legitimacy of Iowa Republicans. But don't count Newt out. A lot of conservatives still view him as the real deal, and some of this negative stuff could very well blow back into the collective faces of those who have dealt it. Keep your eyes as well on one Rick Santorum, whose below-the-radar approach to Iowa, strong organization, and legitimate credentials as a social conservative could put him in the mix as well. Some tell me Santorum could stun Iowa with an out and out come from way behind win!

Expectations for Mitt have come to a new low in Iowa, even with Sunday's endorsement of Romney by the state's largest newspaper, the *Des Moines Register*. By almost any standard this will be a close race for Romney, but a second or close third-place finish would breathe new life into his campaign. Romney's current state of lowered expectations is much easier to meet. Even a surprise win for Mitt is still possible. That's how close it is in Iowa right now.

Listen carefully to the Iowa wind. It's changing, you see, and Newt now finds himself in a tough spot. Although I have always believed that party caucus-goers vote with their hearts and NOT necessarily their heads, there may be some sense among them that this time they can't afford to get it wrong. Watch for one of the following:

1) Paul 2) Gingrich 3) Romney

1) Gingrich 2) Paul 3) Romney

1) Romney 2) Santorum 3) Paul

If these guys are bunched together, then Romney and Gingrich make New Hampshire big game in the stakes for the nomination. I am becoming convinced, however, that the once-moribund Romney operation has suddenly come to life. They can thank Gingrich for that. There's nothing to energize a campaign like a surge from the last guy you would have expected to wake up and bring it on as Gingrich has. Lesson learned: don't run like a frontrunner for two years. It's both presumptive and dangerous! (See Bob Dole.)

The weather is starting to change in New Hampshire as well, and today is especially chilly. Button up and get out your scarves and gloves. This little GOP storm isn't over quite yet. In fact, it's just about to begin. You can feel it in the air.

# THE CAUCUS GAMES:
## *The Iowa Intensity Gap*

There's a thing in early presidential voting contests that has much to do with who wins and who loses. It's at the finish line, where the candidates actually place and show is what distinguishes an actual victory from a perceived one. It's also the silent killer of the political expectations game, which often quietly slips below the polling guru's radar right up until the votes are counted. It is known as the intensity gap, and it has killed many a presumed frontrunner and derailed many a would-be challenger. Simply put: in Iowa there are voters and there are committed voters. Voters have indicated that they will participate in the caucus, but sometimes something just comes up—say a cold spell that might cause hypothermia as one walks from the house to the pickup in the driveway. Committed voters will show up on caucus night no matter the weather, and they will make certain contingency plans to be sure no one gets in their way. There is a huge intensity gap between voters and committed voters in Iowa, especially in this cycle.

The Committeds will arrive early. They'll bring big Iowa farmhands along for muscle in the unlikely event that some volunteer outside in the parking lot tries that age old caucus trick: "Sorry, the church basement is over capacity, fire marshal says no one else inside." Committed caucus-goers know that game. They also know the old "Sorry, no more spaces in the parking lot" trick. That's where that guy with an official-looking blaze orange safety vest and a flashlight stands down the road from the caucus site and directs traffic away from the venue. "No more spaces," the fellow politely tells the uninitiated. "You'll have to drive down the road six miles and park at the Johnson Farm. We'll send the shuttle down in a few minutes to pick you up." For some reason the few rubes who have fallen for that one report they were never picked up! Keep in mind it's usually minus 6 degrees, with a wind chill factor that makes it feel like 40 below. This tends to make these ground games very effective.

In most places we'd call that voter suppression. In Iowa they call it a very good incentive to keep non-committed voters from participating. For this and other reasons, bringing along a couple of corn-fed bouncers makes the more initiated caucus-goers feel they're ensuring themselves and their like-minded friends a seat at the table, as well as a parking space.

Committed voters are angry or frustrated or excited or determined. They collectively run through their drills for caucus night. They recruit friends, relatives, and neighbors. They arrange for babysitters and bring along hot coffee and cocoa in big thermos bottles, along with some homemade snacks just in case their legions become faint on the hypoglycemic sixth ballot.

Committed voters will walk through fire (or snow), because they know the way the game works in Iowa. They also know that they have recruited or spoken with or ride-shared or invited or cajoled or bribed or insisted that a certain number of other committed voters join them. If those folks don't show up, they send the corn-fed bouncers over to their farms to roust 'em and provide transport if necessary. See, voters are country-club participants. If all goes well, if they're not too tired, if they can get the night off from work, or if one of their kids doesn't have a basketball game that night, they'll show up. But those are not the folks who help win caucuses.

This year in Iowa, where's the intensity? It starts with Ron Paul. He's got organization, money, and a clear and slightly unbalanced platform that makes his supporters pretty reliable. Most of them can get to the caucus sites in their spaceships, which also eliminates the potential parking challenges. Paul's ground forces in Iowa are vastly underestimated and no one has factored them into quantitative polling data. Many of these supporters simply don't tell the pollsters the truth (that's part of the fun;

just tell 'em you're undecided!). Look for Ron Paul to over-perform his polling numbers, because he and his forces from the planet Gordar fall largely into the committed voter bloc.

Newt Gingrich, in spite of the pounding he's taken from Paul and from Romney's Super PAC in the mail and on Iowa airwaves for the last couple of weeks, will also have a strong loyal following—although his star has plummeted in the past few days under the weight of tough ads from the Romney Inc. Super PAC. Many of these followers will view the attacks on the former Speaker as an attempt by the franchise to deny Newt the chance to wrestle with Barack Obama in the general election. Look for Newt's voters to over-perform on the intensity scale, making for a close race for a likely 3rd and 4th finish between Gingrich and the Paulitarians. Finally, don't overlook the fact that true Committeds don't give a whit about electability. For them, it's all about ideology, the person they met, the church they attend, and their pastor's favorite. For that reason, Michele Bachmann and Rick Santorum could see surprisingly strong showings. That's because exceeding expectations is part of the committed voters' playbook. There's also Rick Perry, who's (almost) singlehandedly waging a war on Obama's "War on Religion" with spots that attacking almost everything from gays in the military to the introduction of color TV, and chlorination of Iowa's public water supply Perry's appeal to social conservatives can't help him win Iowa, but it too could help him exceed expectations. Remember however, at this point in his campaign, exceeding expectations for Rick Perry means not having his hotel burn down. He's pretty much done! Then, of course, there's Mitt Romney.

Mitt's never been a darling of the social right. He's treated Iowa up until the last ten days as the first human on Mars might view an order from mission control to take a chance and remove his helmet upon first setting foot on the red planet. But Romney is making up for lost time, spending money like a drunken sailor and allying with Paul to put the full Nelson on Newt. Romney is all establishment. But Iowa Republican voters want one thing almost as desperately as a good corn crop next summer, and that is the firing of President Obama. Many friends on the ground in Iowa say there has been a strong feeling that it's time to get going on the President, and that Mitt's the guy who can do it. They claim Mitt will surprise… Maybe even win (they say in a whisper).

Paul, Gingrich, and Romney are fighting for three of the four tickets out of Iowa. Paul, Santorum and to some degree Newt have the committed voters and Mitt's got just a lot of voters. The question is: how many Romney voters fall into the committed column? For Mitt's sake, he'd better hope they don't all wind up re-directed to the Johnson farm, because that would be a bad indicator of the way the night might turn out for him! This will surely be an intense Iowa caucus. In fact this one could be the closest primary in years because in Iowa, intensity matters!

# WON'T YOU BE MY NEIGHBOR:

### *Mister Santorum and Mister Rogers: Separated at Birth?*

There's a lot that can be said about each of the GOP candidates seeking to end Barack Obama's reign of chaos over America. I've certainly said plenty. One candidate that I have barely touched upon is a guy who, for whatever reason, had been the Rodney Dangerfield of the 2012 elephant stampede: Rick Santorum.

Santorum, a former U.S. Senator from Pennsylvania, served two terms in the House and two in the Senate before his defeat in 2006. He is, by almost any standard, a solid, decent, and credible conservative on social and fiscal matters. Santorum reminds voters that he was never one to compromise, and that he worked with others both inside and outside the GOP while he served in Washington to champion a largely fiscal and socially conservative agenda. He invokes the sacred name of Ronald Reagan as much if not more than the other candidates. He apologizes for nothing he believes in today or anything he has ever supported. He also reminds us that his views have never changed. He is rock-solid and committed to the ideals and principles in which he believes.

Santorum has quietly and effectively stuck to the model of retail campaigning long celebrated in early contest states such as Iowa and New Hampshire. He is the only GOP candidate to visit in person each and every one of Iowa's 99 counties, and so far he has made voter interaction at a series of seemingly endless town hall meetings in Iowa and New Hampshire the signature of his campaign.

This is partly due to the fact that Santorum has nowhere near the money it takes to run a Romney-like effort, and has been relegated to campaigning on a budget. He's cheerily flying about the country and racking up more Southwest frequent-flyer points than he'll know what to do with when his campaign ends. Santorum has been both substantive and combative in the GOP debates held since last spring. While he has much to say (when not summarily dismissed or ignored by the moderators), Santorum is by almost any standard the genuine article. Any movement conservative who values the real thing should be flocking to this guy on taxes, on debt, on abortion, on guns, and on foreign policy. There is little in Santorum that a genuine Reagan revolutionary could find fault with.

Yet Santorum continues to languish in the polls in low single digits, unable to break through the craziness of Ron Paul (whom the *Union Leader* of New Hampshire correctly identified in its Sunday editorial as little more than "a gadfly") or the strident edginess of Michele Bachmann. He's been thwarted by the socially conservative king of the political pratfall, Rick Perry. He doesn't have the money or the standing in the polls, and so almost everyone has written the guy off. Not so fast!

While I am not predicting a come-from-behind victory for Santorum in the Hawkeye State, I do believe he will he has the ability to potentially deliver a big surprise on Caucus night. He'll cut into Bachmann, Gingrich, and Perry voters, perhaps just enough in a close race for one of the top two or three spots in Iowa to either change the order or create a more marginal victory for the eventual winner by keeping the front three razor-close. Should this happen, it will quickly re-shape the race and could create yet new conservative alternative to frontrunner Mitt Romney.

Santorum is everything a good underdog should be. He has working-class roots; he was born to a Roman Catholic family with an Italian-immigrant father and a half-Italian, half-Irish mother. Santorum and his wife Karen have seven kids of their own. The campaign has largely been a family effort, with the gang on the road with dad whenever schedules allow. (These kids had better get a trip to Walt Disney World when this thing is through!)

The one mistake Santorum makes again and again, however, is reminding voters that he is the only candidate in the GOP field who has actually won an election in a critical "swing state" While it is a fact that Santorum has won both congressional and statewide elections in Pennsylvania, one of the most important of the swing states, he conveniently omits from his political biography the fact that he also lost his senate seat by a landslide in 2006. In other words, were he currently a sitting Senator, or a guy who left Washington of his own volition, the "I can win in important swing states" argument might have some merit. It does not.

Rick Santorum reminds us all of the guy who lives down the street. The guy we all coached Little League baseball with at some point. The fellow from *Our Town* who you meet on the street where you live or at the dump on Saturday mornings. He's like the guy who shows up for the annual town meeting each year and pleasantly rallies a group of neighbors to help convince the town's highway department to change the expansion of a certain highway to save a 200 year-old oak tree. Rick Santorum, truth be told, is an honorable and decent guy. So decent, in fact, that if you traded his trademark sweater vest for a cardigan, you'd swear he and the late Mister Rogers were very likely separated at birth!

The next time you see Senator Santorum, say hi. Thank him for his service to our country and his principled core beliefs (even if you might not agree with him on everything). Thank him too for his decent, straightforward retail campaign effort. Santorum is, in my book, the happy warrior of the 2012 GOP campaign. All of us are just a little better for the fact that he has been willing to jump into the arena. Who knows? Rick Santorum could deliver the biggest surprise of all by winning the Iowa Caucus and where he goes from there is anybody's guess!

## VERMIN REIGNS SUPREME!:
*The Lesser-known Candidates Debate—*
*A New Hampshire Tradition*

On Monday night, I moderated what has become a small but significantly symbolic event in the New Hampshire presidential primary: The Lesser-Known Candidates Forum. I say important because it represents the chance to show that anyone (and I do mean anyone) who is legally on the ballot in the NH primary and who has not been involved in any of the national televised debates gets a chance at this one event to say his or her piece. This is a chance for these candidates to compare and contrast their own views with those of their better-known colleagues, who have participated so far this cycle in cable debates that have aired more frequently than Seinfeld reruns.

It is a little-known fact that there are 44 candidates on the New Hampshire presidential ballot this cycle, not just the ones you have likely heard about. The First in the Nation Primary is known for being a place that any candidate may run if they: (1) meet the constitutional standards for candidacy (being a natural-born US citizen over the age of 35) and (2) plunk down the $1,000 registration fee with their paperwork with the New Hampshire Secretary of State. A low threshold indeed when you get to meet some of the patriots who file to be official candidates.

The event attracted nine Republicans and seven Democrats to the New Hampshire Institute of Politics at St. Anselm College last Monday evening. The event aired on C-SPAN and was live-streamed on WMUR.com. In addition, there were plenty of other local and national media types there anxious to cover the gritty reality of genuine candidates laid bare: unfiltered and without consultant spin, advance, or security. Each candidate was questioned by panelists Beth Lamontagne Hall from the *Union Leader* and former ambassador Terry Schumaker. The timekeeper for the event was none other than longtime state representative Jim Splaine, the author of the bill that helped ensure New Hampshire's First in the Nation status. The other legend in the room was New Hampshire's diminutive Secretary of State William Gardner, who has met just about all of these folks as they march into his State House office to file their candidacy. The candidates ranged from the interesting to the sublime. Some articulated their positions with great eloquence and thoughtfulness. Question topics ranged from foreign policy to the economy, job creation, and addressing the national debt. To say that these candidates were unscripted would be an understatement, but there they were for all to see, here in the one place in the world where almost anyone has the chance to one day tell their grandkids: "I ran for President!"

Most of the candidates were pleasant and adhered to the time limits given for each response. Some candidates stayed on one particular theme, including Mr. Timothy Brewer, a Republican from Ohio who believes that as President it would be essential for him to communicate with the deceased for guidance on important domestic and foreign policy issues. (Why not? Clearly President Obama's not getting real good advice from the living!)

Another candidate, Mr. Ed O'Donnell, suggested that common decency was the key to all things fundamentally American. He pledged as President to eradicate all guns from the civilian population. This as you might have guessed did not go over real well with New Hampshire's second amendment crowd, and I presumed he would not be getting any support from the guys at the NRA. Then there was a Mr. John Haywood, who argued for a return to the Kennedy/Johnson income tax levels of 1964. I'm not sure what those levels are in today's dollars, but something tells me they would be radically insufficient to support trillion-dollar government bailouts which the current administration seems to think are just dandy! Robert Greene from Lowell, Massachusetts suggested that all of our domestic energy problems could be solved simply by mining Thorium (which apparently is as common as granite around here) and converting it to a refined fuel product. I'm not sure this stuff works or not, but if so I'm hoping my house is sitting on a pile of it. I plan to have the wife and kids join me in digging up the backyard as soon as the frost is out in the spring.

There were several other unique and interesting candidates on the panel. I feel I should mention one Vermin Supreme, a Democrat who refers to himself as a "friendly fascist" and who is an avowed advocate of mandatory tooth-brushing to promote good oral hygiene. As Vermin says, "Strong teeth for a strong America." (If good oral hygiene is really important to Mr. Supreme, I'm betting he drops out at some point and endorses Mitt Romney.) The colorful Mr. Supreme, a "performance artist" and perennial candidate for President, was seated (by alphabetical happenstance) next to one Randall Terry from West Virginia. Mr. Terry is a well-known anti-abortion activist who was part of a bizarre movement known as Operation Rescue a few years back. Mr. Terry was quite vocal during the debate about his anti-abortion and anti-gay rights positions. In a free country and an open forum the man has the right to say what he wants, and this guy did. It became obvious toward the end of the debate, however, that the aforementioned Mr. Supreme took exception to some of Mr. Terry's more strident points. After singing (yes singing!) his closing statement, Mr. Supreme broke the rules, stood from his seat on the dais, and proceeded to cover Mr. Terry in clouds of green glitter, announcing that he was sprinkling "pixie dust" on Mr. Terry and "turning him gay." As photographers came forward to get pictures of the now sparkling Mr. Terry, I gently tried to restore order. All the while Mr. Terry sat, hands folded, adorned in glitter, while Mr. Supreme mugged for the cameras. I must admit it was difficult to maintain my composure and the assembled crowd seemed to love it!

A number of people were angry about Mr. Supreme's antics. To be fair, he didn't exactly play by the rules. But the bottom line is that when you let a bunch of completely unknown people who want to be President of the United States into a room and encourage them in front of lot of cameras to speak their minds and make their case, they do just that and then some. Being insulted when a group like this says or does something unconventional is like feigning shock that wild leopards released from their cages at the zoo ate a few tourists! With free speech comes the risk of an occasional free-for-all, and that's what we got. It was unconventional, different and more than a little bizarre. If you want tight sound bites and rules, spin rooms and handlers, tune into one of the cable or network debates. You can be sure Wolf Blitzer would never allow pixie dust in a CNN debate!

Rock on Vermin!

# CHAPTER THIRTY-ONE

# COUNTDOWN TO A TIE:
### *The Iowa Caucus Results and What They Mean*
### *for the New Hampshire Primary and Beyond*

Just four days to go until Iowa caucus-goers decide who will win, place, and show in the first contest of the 2012 GOP presidential campaign. Right now, things are getting very interesting indeed. The low-expectations game of the Romney campaign in Iowa has provided a nice opportunity in these last weeks for Mitt and his Super PAC to take twenty points out of Newt Gingrich's hide since airing a boatload of tough negative ads against the former House Speaker. In the last twenty days, Gingrich has lost about a point each day as Romney's PAC and Ron Paul's campaign have bombarded Iowa airwaves. The Romney argument is not just about Newt's imperfections as a candidate. Romney now makes a clear and demonstrable point that if Gingrich can fall so precipitously with just a little heat in the Iowa kitchen, think what Barack Obama's billion dollars could do to the Newtster in a general election. Interestingly, the process argument about electability is working for Mitt. There are two words that unite pretty much every faction of the Republican electorate and big chunk of independent voters: "Beat Obama." That's what Mitt is trying to prove he is most capable of doing, and a lot of folks in Iowa are clearly jumping on board.

The flirtation with Gingrich, like the brief dalliances GOP voters have had first with Michele Bachmann, then with Donald Trump, then with Rick Perry, then with Chris Christie, then with Herman Cain, and finally with Newt, have all led back to the same place: the safety and soundness of the very sober Mitt Romney. While Romney has long been the 25 to 30 percent frontrunner, he has kept his eye on the ultimate prize—defeating the President—thereby allowing other flavors of the week to come and go.

The exception to this rule is Gingrich, who scared the Romney high command as he began his comeback surge too close for comfort to the actual voting date. Team Mitt and its Super PAC went to work and rebranded Gingrich as an undisciplined hypocrite who has changed positions more often than he has changed wives, and whose Washington insider status make him part of the problem, not a credible solution. The strongest charge against Gingrich hurled by team Romney is his alleged lobbying for Freddie Mac. That one hit hard and stuck!

Mitt heads into the weekend before the caucus in a much stronger position than even his campaign would have conceded a few weeks ago. He has been "all in" for the last couple of weeks, with actual retail politicking and enough gross rating points on television to more than make a case for himself against Gingrich. Romney cautiously waded into Iowa, the place he wasn't originally going to play this time around. This caution was largely based on the disappointing campaign he ran there in 2008, and the enormous resources he expended. A not-so-secret ground game run by a few of his best lieutenants actually began in Iowa months ago without a lot of fanfare. The Romney campaign appears to have quietly spent significantly on voter contact and turnout efforts for caucus night and right now the intensity gap for Romney seems to be on fire.

If Romney's folks get out the vote and can make impassioned pleas to voters that Mitt can and will defeat Obama, he beats expectations by winning or coming in a close second. That sets up for what appears to be a firewall in New Hampshire, where the former Massachusetts Governor leads with more than 40% of the popular vote as indicated in recent polling. A win in Iowa, and another in New Hampshire, will send Mitt to South Carolina with the political wind and momentum firmly at his back. He's likely to need it south of the Mason-Dixon Line en route to the nomination. Simply put, South Carolina presents a unique set of challenges for the former Massachusetts Governor. However a trifecta win for Romney in Iowa, New Hampshire and South Carolina, as unlikely as it sounds, would mean game, set, match!

But every superhero needs a foil. If Mitt is the caped crusader with money, message, and media, the great hope of the GOP, who better to play villain than the evil Ron Paul? Paul is polling second in Iowa and has a strong and energized organization of fruitcakes who will turn out on caucus night no matter what. Paul's cranky brand of nutty libertarianism is perfect for a Bond villain. He is the Snidely Whiplash to Mitt's Dudley Do-Right. Paul's rhetoric, which includes legalizing pot, ignoring Iranian nuclear ambitions, scrapping the Fed for the gold standard, and building a wall around America, is crazy enough on its own. But then there are those pesky newsletters. The ones with the seething anti-Semitic, racist rhetoric, which immediately suggests the good Dr. Paul may need to have a net thrown over him.

The bad news is the nuts love him! The good news? Thank God there's only a limited number of nuts available. Even if the good doctor should pull out a surprise win in Iowa, he will be quickly set back on his heels in New Hampshire, where he has about as much a shot of winning the Republican primary as I do! Paul continues to play gadfly in this race, making ridiculous comments that make Pat Buchanan's run in 1992 look milquetoast by comparison. (I actually admire Buchanan, even though he gave my former client President George H.W. Bush more than a little heartburn back in the day.)

Paul will do well in Iowa, but something tells me (and this may be my own Pollyanna view of the world) that the people of Iowa are better than Ron Paul. They know for certain that Romney, or maybe even a surging Rick Santorum, are far saner choices for the party. If, however, it is Herr Doktor that Iowa picks, a week later New Hampshire will correct the problem and that will be that. Paul is done after New Hampshire. He's crazy enough to continue on, even maybe threatening a third-party run in the general, which would be a disaster for Republicans and would likely ensure Obama a second term. (While you're looking up crazy in your online dictionary, see Ross Perot!)

The big news for now is that Rick Santorum, the perennial nice guy in the sweater vest, is on the move in Iowa due largely to his bona fide conservative credentials and his 99-county retail campaigning.

Santorum is patient, pleasant, and genuine. He is also unelectable, which means that while he very well may over-perform in Iowa (I see him at least as one of the top three finishers there), the New Hampshire primary will be the necessary reality check to likely send the former Senator back to Pennsylvania or at least back to earth. Got to give the Rickster credit, though: he is the one guy who has kept the retail in this race and has been an honest voice for the conservative cause.

Newt! What can I say, except I really like the guy. Smart, bold, impatient, and unafraid to take risks—sometimes maybe too many. Newt has made this race interesting again, and his comebacks from more than one political near-death experience are still Lazarus-like. Gingrich campaigns without a net. If Romney is safety and soundness, Newt is risky business: bold, and unafraid. Where Mitt is measured and cautious, Newt sees the chance to say something he thought of in the shower that morning. I suppose that the way his mind works, he likely tells himself: "It may be big, bold, and perhaps a bit outrageous. But hey, I've got an audience right now. Why not test-market the idea this very minute?" For Gingrich there are no trial balloons.

Newt has said he could not run a consultant-driven campaign, and that statement could not be truer. Trying to tame the tiger that is Newt Gingrich in terms of message discipline, talking points, and offending as few voters as possible would be a near impossible feat. The very thing that would send me to Betty Ford after the campaign, were I an advisor to Gingrich, is the very thing that makes him most appealing. You have to admire a guy who's bold and honest. It's what makes this circus more exciting. Newt will not do as well in Iowa mainly for the same reasons. He would be a disastrous general-election opponent to the President. Newt peaked about two weeks too early. The clock is running down, and his momentum in Iowa and New Hampshire are going exactly the wrong way.

If there are three tickets out of Iowa, Mitt gets one, Paul gets another (although it's one-way), and Santorum likely gets the third. Michelle Bachman will fly back to her Bat Cave and hang upside down there until it's time for her to get back to Washington and further damage the

GOP brand, much to John Boehner's chagrin. As for Rick Perry—let's just say it's huntin' season in Texas and he'll have plenty of time on his hands real soon to bag plenty of grouse, pheasant, and quail.

Get ready, New Hampshire, because whatever Iowa does on Tuesday, you may well have to set things straight one more time. That is, after all, what a real election is all about.

## JOHN GRISHAM'S NEWEST NOVEL *THE GURU*:
### *Romney Can't Be the Nominee! Can He?*

"A bitter and divisive campaign… that's what we really need," snarled the bespectacled political guru slumped on a couch in the corner of the Obama 2012 campaign headquarters in Chicago. "We need to make Mitt Romney spend the next six months—right up to the convention—defending his right flank against Gingrich or Santorum. That's the ticket. Move him so far to the right that even his wife and kids won't recognize him."

"Could work," said Josh, a smart young staffer carefully tapping every word the guru utters on his shiny new campaign-issued iPad.

"Work?" said the guru. "Of course it will work, as long as we keep Mitt in the far right lane. The Tea Party gang will ultimately never buy Romney as the genuine article, so we'll make him court them, cajole them, flirt, fuss, and bow to them. Just when we get him desperately trying to convince those gun-toting Iowa farmers that he's more Christian than Pat Robertson, Newt or Perry will jump in and remind them that Romney's not real. He's a hoax, a political hypocrite who groveled that he was pro-choice to Bay State voters and even told them that he was for gay rights! This is the stuff that wins elections, Josh. The politics of divisiveness and cynicism. This is our way forward-the road map to re-election."

The guru stood and walked across the room to the floor-to-ceiling windows revealing an impressive view of Michigan Avenue. The late-afternoon traffic wound its way out of the Windy City for the suburbs after another day's grind in a frightened America. The anemic economy had many commuters not going home at all, but to a second or even a third job somewhere to make ends meet. This, the guru knew, was the problem: the economy, the God-damned economy!

"Remember, Josh," he said without turning from the window. "Our guy may be a train wreck, but as long as Romney's not the nominee we will make Santorum or Gingrich—or if there is a God in Heaven—Ron Paul the real issue. If this race is about them, we win. If it's about us, we could very well lose. The only way we lose is if we let Mitt Romney win. That's why we need to crush him now. He needs to lose Iowa and fight for his life in New Hampshire. Then he can limp into the south where Gingrich or Perry will have plenty of like-minded southern conservatives who will not be able to bring themselves to trust Romney. We can make Bain and the Mormon thing finish him off." The guru turned to the young apprentice. "Got it?"

"Yep! I mean yes. Got it. Every word."

"Good. Put it in a memo under my name with the rest of the stuff I emailed you earlier, the stuff on outsourcing jobs, Romney's tax returns and that Swiss bank account tip and send it to the boss in Washington before you leave here tonight. I need it in his hands for a conference call we have with the Big Guy tonight at nine."

"Yes sir!" said Josh, trying to type faster than the guru could talk.

The guru walked from the conference room to his own spacious corner office, where he packed his things in his briefcase and headed to his hotel on the Loop. *This thing is pretty much figured out. Done. Finished. Over,* he thought as he pushed the elevator for the twenty floor descent to street level.

The preceding is not an actual conversation. While it may sound like the first page of a John Grisham novel, you can be sure one or more conversations just like that took place not too long ago and are continuing in Washington and Chicago among "all the President's men." Maybe not all, but the smart ones. The ones who came up with the whole "Hope and Change" thing. The team that designed a campaign that promised to change the tone in Washington.

Their plan for re-election in 2012 was a good one. Deny the best-known, best-financed Republican candidate for President (Romney) a chance to break from his party's most conservative ranks. Isolate him from moderates and independents, swing voters in swing states, economic conservatives and social libertarians. Never would these elements of the Republican base coalesce around Willard "Mitt" Romney. But somehow, some way, it seemed like they were! To the guru's surprise—and to the surprise of many others both in and outside the Republican Party and the Washington beltway—Romney could likely become the franchise Republican candidate for President. Fiscally conservative, a Washington outsider, a business guy who created jobs in the private sector, a Mr. Fix-It. He was selling as "socially conservative enough" to bring the GOP faithful together in Iowa and Libertarian, independents New Hampshire in line as well. The guy the guru thought—hoped—would never have the juice to close the sale raised more money and built the only national campaign organization of the 2012 GOP field.

Romney was, it appeared, on the verge of winning, or at the very least making a strong showing in Iowa. He also seemed poised to seal the deal with a double-digit lead in New Hampshire. The candidate the guru and President Obama feared the most was perhaps on the cusp of wrapping up the GOP nomination before the President even delivered his mid-January State of the Union address. South Carolina: Maybe. But Florida: Romney. Nevada: Romney. And on it would go, "*Shit*," muttered the guru as the elevator doors opened, revealing the sterile but congested lobby of the Chicago office tower and its swarm of worker bee's spilling from the elevator cars and headed for the street. This would be a long night, a long campaign... too long.

✶ ✶ ✶ ✶ ✶

No votes have actually been cast yet. As with baseball, it's tough to call the game before the first batter gets to the plate. But Romney and company have done three things in this campaign far better than I initially gave them credit for:

1.  They knew they needed to run a national campaign and assumed that someone else might too. They did. No one else could.

2.  Romney, Inc. knew that if they were vulnerable to flip-flops and evolving positions, their opponents were far weaker on a myriad of personal, political, and ideological challenges. If Romney's camp needed to exploit their opponents' foibles, they could quickly and effectively with a few thousand gross rating points and a little direct mail (see Newt Gingrich). They also were stunned to learn that the field was so weak. Bachmann flamed out after the Ames Straw Poll. Perry was like a NASA launch that went terribly, tragically wrong. Cain was never ready for his close-up and had a few alleged tawdry personal issues that surfaced. Ron Paul was, well, Ron Paul. Even the guru knew well that the luxury of facing Ron Paul as the GOP standard-bearer was simply too good to be possible. Then there was Santorum: the last guy to finally get a little respect in Iowa. Good guy, worked hard, earned a place in Iowa, maybe even a win. But where would he go from there? The answer: probably nowhere, but who really knows?

3.  Romney Inc. created the answer to the one thing every Republican voter really and truly wanted this year just in time for Christmas: a candidate from outside Washington who actually had a life outside politics. Someone who made tough choices in the private sector, where real jobs are created. A guy who turned around the Olympics and got himself elected the Republican Governor of the single most Democratic state in America. If Romney could appeal to Massachusetts voters enough to be elected Governor, then the guys at Romney Inc. would, as Captain Picard from Star Trek would say, "make it so"— again.

So here we are on the eve of the Iowa caucus. Romney Inc. has done a masterful job of downplaying expectations until just the last day or so in Iowa. If Mitt comes in a close second or wins—especially against a lunatic like Ron Paul, or a guy who likely can't win the nomination or general election like Santorum—it is a moral victory by any measure. With Newt Gingrich near mortally wounded, courtesy of pro-Romney Super PAC knife work and Paul's incessant attacks, and with Perry and Bachmann now beginning to think about getting back to their day jobs after South Carolina, Romney might have clear sailing all the way to the nomination. But there will, no doubt, be bumps along the road for Mitt. Barring some unforeseen catastrophe or unimaginable mistake, Mitt Romney is about to seal the GOP deal in what could be the shortest time period from the Iowa caucus in modern presidential campaign history. The long-opined listless frontrunner strategy that Romney Inc. appeared to be executing was better than anyone thought. Either that, or these guys are very lucky. I think it's likely a bit of both.

 And right now, in the gathering darkness on the 20th floor of a gleaming downtown Chicago office tower, the guru is likely sitting with young Josh nearby. The guru is thinking out loud about the next steps and the general election. Josh is typing so fast that the guru actually becomes annoyed, distracted by his thumping gyrations on the touchscreen of the iPad. This has not worked out the way they anticipated. Romney appears to be pulling this thing off. It's time to call Washington and get to work on Plan B.

# IOWA SAVES ITSELF FROM IRRELEVANCE (BARELY):

*And Then There Were Four: Romney, Santorum, Gingrich… and Paul's Still Hanging Around Too!*

The people of Iowa have spoken. In a historic presidential caucus the result is… a tie! It was a fascinating night to watch Mitt Romney, Rick Santorum, and Ron Paul battle it out for the top spot in the quadrennial Hawkeye ritual. It still stuns me to imagine that at the end of a long night something like eight votes separated Mitt Romney and Rick Santorum. Both achieved stunning victories. Santorum's shoestring campaign was all retail, no glitz. It was as retail as it could be with the candidate and a small cadre of loyal followers. Santorum is the everyman's social conservative, a retro Ronald Reagan in a sweater vest. Iowa was fertile soil for Santorum's brand of social conservatism, and he deserves his moment in the sun for a stunning come-from-behind tie with Romney.

Mitt, on the other hand, had his own big win in Iowa. Overcoming tamped-down expectations, and winning a state that was not in his political wheelhouse ideologically speaking, Romney proved that there is in fact a certain momentum and inevitability to his long road to the GOP nomination. Some pundits and pretty much every White House spinner spent the night pointing out that Romney's Iowa showing was statistically less impressive than his showing there in the 2008 caucus. Give me a break! Different field, different time, different election! If nothing else, the Democrat spin machine showed it is in fact very much concerned about facing Romney in the general election.

Then there's Ron Paul. A close third, Paul cobbled together a coalition of younger voters looking to legalize pot and a bunch of isolationists whose view of reality (especially as it relates to foreign policy and America's place in a dangerous and complex world) is, let's say, disconcerting. At least Iowans were able to put a couple of points between crazy Uncle Ron and the Romney-Santorum tie. Close, yes, but the results tell us that caucus-goers are smart enough to sort the wheat from the nuts!

Now the circus arrives in New Hampshire, where the candidates face a different electorate in a real election. Republicans and Independents will decide New Hampshire, and Romney's organization, franchise, brand strength, money, message, and media will be hard to overcome. Santorum faces the bright spotlight of suddenly finding himself in the money coming out of Iowa. With Perry headed back to the ranch, and Bachmann not long for this race, Santorum, if he stays real, could be the target of a whole lot of scrutiny from the Romney/Paul folks and their Super PAC friends. Get ready for seven days of ugly in the Granite State. The stakes in New Hampshire have been raised significantly based on Iowa's punt.

Then there's Newt Gingrich. Newt is mad. Newt is frustrated. Newt pulled off a concession attack speech in Iowa where he went right for the Romney jugular. The *Union Leader* newspaper is in New Hampshire and they are with Newt, but expect more than just tough editorials from the paper. Newt will create his own artillery barrage this time, and I'm guessing it won't be pretty.

Say this for Iowa: Paul came close, but he didn't win. Now it's left to New Hampshire to sort things out. If Romney wins here it's pretty much done. Paul's not going anywhere soon, no matter what happens, as he really doesn't have much else to do. The role of gadfly must be filled by someone. The real question is whether Santorum can survive the white-hot heat of finding himself at least for now in the money. Is he real or was Iowa just a fluke? Can he convince voters he's more than a one-state wonder? Or, as I suspect, is Rick Santorum the Mike Huckabee of 2012, with a slightly less impressive vote total in Iowa than Huckabee achieved? In any event, on to New Hampshire. Please get this sorted out.

# HELP WANTED:
### *Assistance from Needed Super PACs in New Hampshire NOW*

Male, GOP candidate for President, 64, financially well-off, good family, excellent hair and strong political franchise, seeks assistance from well-funded, generous, like-minded, and unaffiliated Super PAC's in helping to negatively "define" little-known fellow from Pennsylvania.

Subject is a 6-foot white male, socially conservative, traveling with wife and a bunch of kids. He is a former U.S. Senator who appeals to evangelical Christian conservatives with strong family values. Interested PACs and/or special interest groups must be willing to provide significant negative contrast advertising (TV preferred, direct mail also appreciated) to keep subject from getting too much gravity with New Hampshire Republican primary voters.

Interested Super PACs should not respond to this want ad. Just do the right thing. Suggested on-air spends: WMUR-TV, Boston TV, maybe even a little Portland and Burlington stuff just to seep into the North Country and the western part of the Granite State. Cable spends also encouraged. Qualified Super PACs should be prepared to spend 1,200 to 1,500 GRPs a week at minimum.

Ads should be tough. Topical suggestions for consideration: earmarking during Senate career, losing senate re-election in critical swing state, and the fact that subject is not ready to go the distance against Obama (just suggestions of course).

Opposition research available upon request. Will be dropped off at Boston's Back Bay T station (left on second bench from doorway at pre-arranged time) in plain brown envelope with the words "Project Keystone" written in black marker. Please arrange for drop-off time by leaving your disposable cell phone number with "Jake" at the Green Unicorn Bar and Bowl in Quincy, Massachusetts.

All interested parties will be kept strictly confidential. Your discretion greatly appreciated.

# DEAR MR. PRESIDENT (PART II):

*Another Secret Memorandum to President Obama*
*from Chief Political Strategist (and Guru) David Axelrod*

As the New Hampshire primary approaches, once again I can't help but to think what Team Obama is thinking about now. It might look a little like this:

Memorandum to: POTUS
From: David Axelrod
Date: January 6, 2012
Re: New Hampshire GOP Primary

Nice job yesterday, sir, gutting the military! A brilliant stroke! Sends just the right message to that pre-pubescent heir apparent to the ill will of North Korea. I'll bet the Iranian's and the Pakistanis are also pleased. Israel will likely not sleep well tonight, but don't worry, our numbers are pretty solid on the capturing and killing terrorists issue. That should hold us for a while. Speaking of possible threats of extremists to our American way of life...

Our folks on the ground in New Hampshire report some interesting stuff indeed. Since the rubes in Iowa made their caucus ritual a tie, the elephants have begun eating their young. Now I know we never planned for Romney to win or even tie the cornfield follies, but he did. I'm not sure what's stranger: that Romney was able to not be embarrassed, or that Rick What's-His-Name came out of nowhere. In any event, the menagerie has officially settled in New Hampshire and things are going pretty well.

As I predicted, Gingrich is attacking Romney as a "Massachusetts moderate," and he's got an ad on the air that whacks the "Mittster" pretty hard. Romney's Super PAC is still hitting Gingrich here and in South Carolina. They clearly want to be sure this vampire doesn't come back to life. (I use this reference because I have in fact seen all of the *Twilight* movies, and vampires are very cool right now.) There's another rumor here that the press has been all over today. Supposedly Gingrich and Rick What's-His-Name are in cahoots against Romney. The campaigns both deny this non-aggression pact, but the conspiracy theorists in the mainstream media love this. They're all following it with great interest, just as instructed.

Gingrich and... Santorum, that's it. Newt said that on the whole welfare reform thing Santorum was akin to the "junior partner at a law firm." Santorum has made it clear that when he and Gingrich disagree he will not be afraid to say so. Both campaigns are whispering that the final two debates here may just be a slugfest. Clearly Newt and Santo reserve the right to throw punches at each other. Santorum has raised over $2 million in the last couple of days. If he can turn that into some gross rating points on air I sense the possibility of a little challenge perhaps. Ron Paul's been MIA, but he arrives here tomorrow tanned, rested, and ready to keep the zany going in the GOP through this winter scrum. Huntsman? No pulse, but he does take points out of Romney's hide. So long as he stays right here he's bound to at least have something to show. Even though Bachmann is out, Perry is somehow still in. But the Romney alternatives are quickly dropping off the radar.

Speaking of non-aggression pacts, Mitt was endorsed by John McCain at a couple of low-energy, flat-tire events that frankly made an exhausted Romney look pretty bad. Things were a little better yesterday, and he and Johnny Mac have headed to South Carolina for the day. While the polling numbers have yet to move here, I have a sense they are about to. It is clear that Gingrich is damaged goods. He is also pretty cranky, and a cranky Newt will do little to rehabilitate his brand.

Santorum, however, does have a little bit of juice since Iowa, but his campaign is having a hard time pivoting from Iowa to new Hampshire and I'm betting he finishes 3rd or 4th here. There's no way Santorum can win in New Hampshire but I get the sense the press wants something to write about.

This weekend, the story is going to be that he's moving up and closing the gap. Frankly, I'm betting he doesn't end up giving Romney much of a scare. All Santorum needs is a respectable second place. If somehow he can even get close to Romney he will claim victory and head south to friendlier ideological territory, presumably with more money. You see, sir, the press has built the Romney expectation here so high that anything less than a 30-point win is a loss! At least that's what our guys have been spinning. Bottom line, Romney will still win here, but the plot will thicken because some conservatives still want a conservative alternative to Mitt. We all know what's waiting for him in South Carolina!

I'm sending you this after a long day for both of us. While you were dismantling America's military establishment, we were busy attempting to dismantle the Republican frontrunner. I would say we have both made good progress. I will update you as necessary. Welcome home and Happy New Year!

PS: Not sure if you own a sweater vest, but I would pick up a couple of them next time you and Michelle are at Target. They have become very popular on the campaign trail. If Santorum can rock one, so can you. You're much cooler-even cooler than vampires!

# THE GRANITE STATEMENT:
## *The Party's Over, and the Elephants Head South*

New Hampshire saw an early and decisive finish to what had been a nearly eight-year effort by Mitt Romney to capture the GOP nomination for President. It ended with the former Massachusetts Governor garnering just under 40% of First in the Nation votes cast, leaving 16 points between he and Texas gadfly/quadrennial candidate, Congressman Ron Paul. Paul's strong showing here is important, because nothing says "strong GOP" like a good showing for a short cranky old guy who wants us to isolate America from the rest of the world and carry gold bars for currency (that's a convenient way to try to feed a parking meter). Paul gave his concession/victory speech in a rambling 20-minute rant, complete with two guys standing behind him with Spock haircuts and matching eyeglasses who looked like they were beamed down from an East Berlin techno bar.

The rest of the pack was far behind. Jon Huntsman fell significantly short of the surge he was feeling in the final days here in New Hampshire, with just under 17% of the vote. He had camped out here in NH with his wife and family, and narrowly avoided having to pay property taxes for his time spent domiciled in the "Live Free or Die" state.

Newt Gingrich got just 9% in spite of strong support from the *Union Leader*, which lent him its endorsement just as his November surge began. Mr. Speakah has become grumpy and bitter after his poor showing in Iowa and a trouncing from the Romney-friendly Super PAC. Memo to Newt: Bitter, angry and cynical is no way to campaign for President. I assume Newt will hang around for a while, bashing Romney for being a capitalist until either a) he runs out of money or b) Callista runs out of hair spray—whichever comes first! South Carolina is likely the first place Newt may be able to muster the Southern flank and actually win the primary there.

Finally, former Senator Rick Santorum placed right there with Newt with 9%, putting to rest once and for all that age-old fashion question: does the sweater vest make the man? The answer: a definitive NO.

Mitt gave a rousing victory speech with plenty of Romney Inc. cameras rolling for a new series of TV spots. Mitt was looking presidential, and his aim was not at his GOP rivals, but squarely at the President. That's smart. The Romney guys have taken a lot of guff from me and others over the last few months for running what many believed has been a lackluster, imperial campaign. In the end, however, they did everything right by effectively navigating the tricky waters of a GOP primary with a big-name brand like Mitt. Team Romney should be proud, and I believe if Mitt survives South Carolina (doubtful), he wins Florida. That could be all she wrote. After the Palmetto State, Huntsman's done (if he even gets there), Santorum could be done, and Newt is well done— maybe even burned to a proverbial crisp unless of course redemption comes in a Dixie victory for the speaker which is quite possible.

Texas Governor Rick Perry's clock was cleaned in Iowa, so he went to Texas to reassess. Apparently he saw some kind of apparition the next morning while jogging, which made him decide to play in South Carolina. He will lose there, joining Gingrich in an inexcusable attack on free-market capitalism, which until now has been a hallmark virtue of the GOP. He'll likely head home after coming in fifth or sixth there, as-suming he can remember where he parked his car.

There was another player in Tuesday's battle, and it was the New Hampshire primary itself. Some of the national press thought it was dull. They called it a snoozer because of the certainty of a Romney win. But the fact still remains: Iowa winnows the field, while New Hamp-shire punches tickets to the next contest and beyond. There were three tickets punched in New Hampshire: Romney, Paul, and Huntsman. But six will go on to South Carolina, creating a nasty spitting match aimed at Romney and one another. As long as Ron Paul, Gingrich, Perry, and Santorum stay in the race, no other candidate will garner a plurality of votes, thereby allowing Mitt to begin in earnest the road to the nomination.

New Hampshire proved once again that their Republicans, much like those in the rest of the nation, prefer name-brand candidates to the less-expensive generics. Romney now joins an historic cadre of franchise Republicans, including Dole, the Bushes, and McCain, who were validated by Granite Staters. The fun's just beginning, and New Hampshire will remain in play as a critical swing state in the general election. The contrast between Romney and the President could not be clearer. Voters will need to make a simple choice: four more years of Obama, or a new start with Romney? They'll figure it out like they usually do. And maybe, just maybe, we'll get it right this time. Because this time it's not about hope and change, it's about the competence and very future of our Republic.

# CHAPTER THIRTY-SEVEN

# CHRIS MATTHEWS MEETS THE WRATH OF SUNUNU:

### *John H Sununu is One of the Best Parts of Presidential Politics!*

I have a number of favorite moments from the week of the New Hampshire Primary, but I must say one of the highlights was watching my old friend and political godfather, former Governor John H. Sununu, take on Comrade Chris Matthews and the rest of the Polit Bureau crowd from MSNBC. A few things about Sununu:

He's smart. Very smart.

He's tough. Nobody ever referred to John H. Sununu as the "Luv Guv."

He does not suffer fools gladly! JHS will say it once and assume that you understand English and that his point has been made, especially if you are a left-leaning mainstream media type.

Sununu is impatient. If you don't get it the first time, he might (and I say might) slowly repeat himself to ensure that you have fully absorbed his point. Make sure you get it the second time.

John H. Sununu is fearless. He cares not who he offends if the party questioning him is either not listening or trying to goad him into some rhetorical question.

John Sununu once referred to himself as a pussycat. That was sarcasm.

Sununu has great strategic ability, a highly analytical mind, sharp political instincts, and he's understandably cynical about those on the left. Sununu live is like watching the Great Wallendas "Walk the Wire" 100 stories above the ground without a net or a safety harness. That's what makes Sununu such good TV.

Sununu had a couple run-ins this past week with a few stupid left-leaning TV commentators, and they were vintage Sununu! The first live exchange took place at a Romney event with comrades Chris, Howard Fineman, and Eugene Robinson all safely attached to the anchor desk at MSNBC's Communist Central Command headquarters at the Radisson Hotel in Manchester, NH. The Governor was doing a live shot in the back of a huge crowd at a Romney rally, with at least a thousand supporters behind him. He had trouble hearing a series of questions from the MSNBC clowns that could have been written by one of Stalin's press lackeys. This only added to the fun. The apparent delay in his earpiece and the noise in the hall made for awkward moments while Sununu processed the baited questions for the pap they truly were. Once John H. understood the setup question, he quickly called out the foolishness, leaving Comrade Chris and his henchmen stunned and speechless.

Matthews started on the issue of Super PACs, attempting to force Sununu to admit that the whole legal but flawed *Citizen's United* ruling by the Supreme Court was actually a secret deal engineered by Team Romney.

Matthews: "Governor Sununu, should candidates be responsible for ads put on by the air by their former staffers and friends in their interests? Should they be responsible for the content of those ads?" (Smile and sneer, as only Matthews can.)

Sununu: "Look, you guys are wallowing in a ridiculous perception of what's going on! Come on, stop being ridiculous and get to the point. You guys don't even understand New Hampshire politics!" (POW!)

Matthews: "I was in Iowa, and couldn't get away from the ads run by your candidate." (Comrade Chris was clearly referring by the hit jobs the Romney-friendly Super PAC had made against Newt Gingrich in Iowa, not the Romney campaign itself.)

Sununu: (Interrupting.) "There's nothing wrong with them!"

Matthews: "Saturating with negativity and then saying he's not responsible..."

Sununu: "He's not!" (Now he's getting a tad angry. I'm seeing that familiar Sununu nostril flare. Part of me wants to warn the Politburo that they might want to back off (John Sununu mad is not pretty). He continued above the din of the crowd, "Do you even know what the law is? You guys have an agenda you want to drive and you have no idea what the rules and regulations are that all these candidates are following! Come on!" (BAM!)

Matthews: (Now he's getting frustrated and embarrassed at this public spanking. No one talks that way to Comrade Chris! He rolls his eyes.) "Let me ask you one last time, do you think the [Super PAC] law is a good law that allows candidates to destroy their opponents without a signature?"

Sununu: (Steam from ears is now becoming slightly apparent.) "Of course not! Every candidate agrees the law should be changed! Nobody likes that law, but unfortunately bad legislation put the Supreme Court in a position where they had to make a bad decision!" (WHAMMO!)

The foolishness continued as The *Washington Post*'s Eugene Robinson attempted to pile on Sununu, only to be put in his place to the point where the poor guy got caught on a cut-away sheepishly looking at Matthews for reinforcements after Sununu let him have it! At various points I found myself cheering at the TV. How many times have you yelled at Chris Matthews's foolishness? Now Sununu was there to speak for all of us, and speak he did!

The exchange went on. Matthews at one point criticized Mitt Romney for being an evil capitalist at Bain & Company, then suddenly changed course and tried to goad Sununu into admitting that Romney was "a career politician."

Sununu's response was classic: "You guys have got to decide whether you want to attack him for being a career politician or attack him for all the success he had as a career private sector guy. How can you be a career both?"

The fun got even better a few nights later as election results streamed in, giving Romney what would be a 16-point win in New Hampshire. This time Sununu was live from Romney headquarters, and the commotion and mob of supporters in the background made it even harder to hear the MSNBC questioners in their full liberal panic. Why MSNBC decided to allow another dose of the full Sununu on air is beyond me, but the Governor was even better on election night. He was buoyed by Romney's impressive showing and clearly tired of stupid questions from the Main Stream Media—especially the loon's at MSNBC. This time it was on of all programs, Rachel Maddow's gabfest.

Ed Schultz (that arbiter of neutrality and fairness) posed a question to Sununu about an alleged "study" from some group of general malcontents known as the Tax Policy Center. This group, Schultz informed Sununu, studied Mitt Romney's economic plan and came to the conclusion that the Romney plan would raise taxes on Americans making less than $40,000, but would cut taxes on millionaires by 5%.

Sununu interrupted Comrade Schultz. "Who? Where did that study come from?" Fast Eddie tried again repeating the stupid question and citing the group responsible for "the study"… Sununu smiled. "With all due respect to that organization, there's a technical term for that: it's a crock of crap!" I, along with millions of Americans, let out a collective gut laugh. Schultz went back in his hole. Sununu next went on to deal with Lawrence O'Donnell's foolishness about Romney's win being less impressive than President George H. W. Bush's win in the 1992 NH Primary. This was supposed to be an indicator that Romney was "weak." Sununu schooled Larry, reminding him that then-President Bush was a sitting President. "You're grasping at straws!"

Watching these two exchanges, I began to remember why I like and respect Governor Sununu so much. He's a guy who shoots from the hip, and there could be no more loyal or articulate advocate for the Republican cause than he. Some people still might underestimate John H. Sununu, but they do so at their own peril. That's because he's unafraid to say what he thinks and to call it like he sees it. Especially when it's nothing more than "a crock of crap!"

# DEAR MR. PRESIDENT (PART III):
*The Latest Secret Memorandum to President Obama from Chief Political Strategist David Axelrod*

As the final critical early primary fast approaches, I can only dream of what the community organizer-in-chief is being told about the facts on the ground. I imagine he might be receiving reports like this:

Memo: To POTUS
From: The Ax Man
Date: Thursday, January 18
Subject: Newt and Mitt Going Nuclear in Dixie

Sir, just a quick update from our trackers in the field who have been embedded with our GOP enemies in South Carolina; First, remember all that "Romney is going to be the guy" stuff we told you after New Hampshire? Things might be changing a scootch. Not sure if you caught the GOP debate the other night from the Golf Course World, but Mitt got beat up pretty badly. Made Tebow's thudding from Brady look meager. Mitt was not on his game either! Newt was very strong, and the crowd seemed to eat it up, especially his response to the race-baiting stuff from our new FAF (Friend at Fox) Juan Williams! There was a whole lot of Southern hootin' and hollerin' going on in that arena, which makes me feel like the new south might just behave like the Old South in Saturday's primary.

If Gingrich beats Romney here, a state that in recent history has always picked the eventual GOP nominee, we could be in for one hell of a good time in Florida. I'm thinking you may want to book a trip down to Disney for a few days with Michelle and the girls. Newt looks like he may just emerge as the Anti-Mitt from hell, which means two things: 1) Santorum is done. If you need a grey sweater vest they will be on clearance on Sunday. 2) Newt could lead the right flank of the Grand Old Party against Romney for the nomination, producing exactly what we had hoped for: a long and arduous fight for the nomination. We may want to put a few Newt attacks up online just to soften him up a tad after Florida. We made 6,450 of them just in case, so there are lots of options.

Romney's problems are the old ones just plaguing him in reruns. Newt's class warfare thing (which he stole directly from us, by the way) seems to be working pretty well. Bain Capital is starting to look like Enron only meaner, and Romney is actually beginning to resemble Ebenezer Scrooge in some of the attack ad… It's amazing how well the Gingrich people took our advice and carpet-bombed the guy because for being successful. This class warfare idea of mine is more brilliant than we even realized! On top of that, Mitt has not released his tax returns, and says he likely won't until after they are finished for this tax year. That's really helped our cause, as he has also had to admit that his personal tax rate was just 15%, which is less than the average middle-class voter and works nicely into our one percent narrative.

With just three days to go, I wanted you to know that Romney may blow South Carolina! Relax, sir, things are working exactly as planned. We got all the spots done on him for the general, and Nancy Pelosi is prepared to run around the country with that video of she and Newt on the loveseat to hold pressers wherever we send her. Also, we found a bunch of former GOP house members with no love for Gingrich who have agreed to endorse us if he is the nominee. We've also found a couple of our pals over at Freddie Mac, who hired Newt to be their historical consultant just about the time they went bust and caused a good chunk of America to lose their homes! Seems like we may have caught ourselves a real break here sir. I will keep you apprised of things as we get more.

I have prepared a mass mailing of thank-you notes to the GOP in South Carolina in the event they hand us Newt on a silver platter. These are good God-fearing folks who deserve our appreciation. We have loaded up the auto-signature machine with fresh ink so that you will be able to sign each one personally!

# SOUTH CAROLINA, Y'ALL COME BACK NOW:
### *It's Now or Never for Mitt!*

That loud noise you heard Saturday evening around seven was the collective primordial scream of the South Carolina GOP indicating that they were in no mood to coronate Mitt Romney with their party's presidential nomination—at least not yet and not here in the heart of Dixie. Romney Inc. was trounced by Newt Gingrich in the Palmetto State, with Newt racking up support from nearly every segment of the GOP electorate. He won with social and religious conservatives. He won with economic conservatives. He won with voters who felt they had been left behind by Obama's policies. According to exit polling, Gingrich even won among female voters (married and single), which seems to suggest that even though the former Mrs. Gingrich was troubled by Newt's request for an open marriage, the women of South Carolina apparently weren't terribly concerned.

Newt's win was not unexpected, and South Carolina is a conservative bastion well-suited to his bona fides. But so too was Iowa, where Romney won (then apparently lost when a couple of hayseed precinct captains finally turned in their caucus tallies after they were half-eaten by someone's barn goat). In any event, the Mitt Romney who campaigned in South Carolina was a very different candidate than the one who surprised a lot of us by exceeding expectations among the fried-butter evangelicals of corn country. The Mitt we saw this past week had lost his mojo. He was defensive, uncomfortable with the idea of being pegged by his opponents as wealthy and successful, and timid and out of touch (to use Newt's words) when it came to defending capitalism and free markets. Romney bumbled through two debates without articulating and defending the fundamental premise of his candidacy: private sector experience. Aside from that, he was also unable to counter-punch Newt's Obama-esque attacks on Bain Capital and market capitalism in general. His wimpy "maybe" when he was asked in the second South Carolina debate by CNN's John King if he would release his tax returns was so bad, he was loudly booed in the debate hall. Those of us watching at home shook our heads and assumed he was just plain giving up!

Gingrich didn't so much win South Carolina as Romney lost it. Mitt was up in SC polls by double digits after his big win in New Hampshire, and then lost the primary by 12 points.

Gingrich, on the other hand, has figured out his narrative and engineered yet another comeback from the political dead, while taking the kind of fire few candidates could ever hope to survive. Here is a guy who is interesting and bright, but also the most personally and politically flawed GOP candidate to seek the presidency ever! Think about it: 40-plus years in the toxic city that is Washington. He was ejected from the House Speakership by his own party after a reprimand for ethics violations. This guy took $1.5 million from Freddie Mac, the quasi-government-run mortgage giant that screwed a bunch of Americans out of their homes and helped push the housing bubble into near sub-prime extinction. Newt was a "historian" for Freddie? Sure he was. Newt and his firm, the Gingrich Group, are lobbyists plain and simple. While the Speaker himself may not be a registered lobbyist, members of his firm sure are. As Yogi Berra would say: "You can look it up!"

Last week wife number two, Marianne Gingrich, explained to ABC's Brian Ross that Newt, who was having an affair with his current wife Callista (the Stepford wife glued to his side at every campaign appearance these days), apparently asked for an open marriage! You can't make this stuff up! But during the CNN debate, when King led off the debate with a question about the open marriage allegations, Newt lit into him like a blowtorch for demeaning the process with such drivel! The crowd loved it. King looked defeated. Newt won the debate before it even started.

Unlike Mitt Romney, Newt knows his weaknesses as well as his strengths, and he plays well to both. He knows attacking the media works with GOP voters. Everyone knows that they're all in the tank for Obama. Reminding the base that Newt's on to them is always good for a solid applause line from the GOP faithful. Newt also knows that he is no saint. He openly admits that he's made mistakes in his life. He's matured and grown, found Callista, re-discovered his daughters from his marriage to his first wife. He has wonderful grandchildren. Oh yes, and he discovered the Lord somewhere in there and found Catholicism, which has made him a changed man.

When he attacks Romney, he claims it's not because he doesn't like the guy, or that he's trying to wreck the party. It's because he wants to fully vet the Governor so that the GOP doesn't nominate a guy whose tax returns or self-admitted commitment to success by practicing capitalism might hurt in the general election. It's a circuitous but effective offense and defense. Newt likes to finish with his ability as a good debater. The argument is that he and only he can take on the great and powerful Obama in a series of Lincoln/Douglas-style debates in the general election. Then he proves that he's good by kicking Mitt's ass! (By the way, don't count on Obama showing up to those Lincoln/Douglas debates.)

Newt's also got some great populist stuff that really works with GOP primary voters, especially those of the more conservative variety. He contrasts himself effectively against Obama by saying, "Barack Obama has been the most effective food stamp President in American history. I would like to be the best paycheck President in American history." How about this one? "You can be sure that if I'm elected never again will you see a U.S. President bow before a Saudi King!" The crowd roars. And then there's Newt's newest line from the populist playbook, one he introduced during his victory speech as he began to focus on Florida: "We don't want to run a Republican campaign, we want to run an AMERICAN campaign. I ask you to be with me, not just FOR me." The crowd goes wild!

So what can Mitt do? First, get back to the fundamental premise of his candidacy: that he is the guy from outside Washington who fixes stuff that's broken. He did it at Bain and was so good at it that he made himself and a lot of other people a boatload of money. In the process, he created successful companies that have sustained real private-sector jobs and employed middle-class workers. When Newt or some other Beltway hack suggests Romney "laid off" workers and was, as the late Rick Perry once called him, "a vulture capitalist," Mitt should respond by saying:

"Of course you guys are gonna say this stuff. You've never run anything besides a bureaucracy in your lives, and you have never fixed anything. When you risk private capital and you succeed, your success is rewarded. At Bain, we put money up for troubled companies that needed our help, management direction, and financial capital. Most of the time we were successful. Some of the time we were not. That's how free enterprise works. Everyone who owns their own business, be it a large company or a small family operation, knows that you live with risk in the real world every day. We were in the business of creating jobs.

"Of Course we had to lay off some people. That's because despite our best efforts some of the companies we acquired were simply not sustainable. They couldn't survive as world markets, technology, demand, costs, market forces, and manufacturing models changed. When things don't work out in the private sector you need to be able to make tough decisions. You can't just kick the can down the road for the next generation of management or owners to deal with as we do in the Federal government. I've made plenty of tough calls and it's not easy. It's just a fact. It's not like Washington where you can ignore entitlement programs that are broken and just keep trying to fool people. I come from a different place than Speaker Gingrich and President Obama. They've been doing it their way in Washington for a very long time, and look where it's gotten us: record deficits, trillions in debt, and Americans who actually believe that if we don't fix this mess their kids will not have the same opportunities as they did. It's time to fix this mess once and for all. I'm the one guy tough enough, smart enough, and confident enough to approach this the way it's done in the real world.

I will eliminate whole departments in Washington that waste our tax dollars and saddle the hardworking people of this country with bureaucracy and regulations that have become unbearable and smother our economy. The way you close federal agencies is to have the guts to fundamentally re-structure Washington. Yes, that's going to mean pink slips for some bureaucrats. I've done it before, and I'll do it again! It's how I created over a hundred thousand sustainable private-sector jobs. It's how I fixed the Olympics. It's how I cut taxes in Massachusetts, balanced the budget, and did it as a Republican in a state filled with Democrats. Now is not the time to continue deluding ourselves with the weak and wimpy age-old solutions offered by the Washington way. Washington stopped working a long time ago. It's time to do it a different way: the American way. If Speaker Gingrich and the President want to defend the status quo that they've built and been a part of in Washington, that's their choice. I, along with the rest of the American people, have run out of patience waiting for Washington to fix things with bigger government, more spending, and no accountability. My America—our America—is too great to be stewarded by the old Washington solutions. The time has come for a new approach, a bold new direction that will allow every American a shot at the American dream: building a small business or finding and keeping a reliable private-sector job in a country that is once again the economic engine that leads the world. If you like the status quo, stay with Gingrich and Obama. If you want a revolution, then let's start one together!"

That's the Mitt Romney we need to see in Florida now! Newt's ticket to Disney World will cause a world of hurt for the GOP and the country if he continues with his cynical, snide, and dare I say un-Republican philosophy of attacking capitalism. The time has come for Governor Romney to stand tall and remember the reason he got into this race in the first place: to offer a new direction away from Obama and Newt. The two are now one, and Mitt needs to let everyone know it. Let's go, Governor. We're counting on you.

# JURASSIC FLORIDA:
## *Mitt Romney is Spoiling Newt's Tropical Vacation!*

It seems that the Sunshine State may just step up and do the right thing in the GOP primary on Tuesday. While the race is still close by most polling measures, it appears that Floridians have come to understand what's on the line in this election. Mitt Romney may not be perfect, but he's the best candidate to nominate if the GOP hopes to send President Obama packing in November. Why has Florida processed this race so deliberately and responsibly so far?

First, Florida is very different from South Carolina, from both a demographic and an issues matrix standpoint. The state's Republican party has become markedly more conservative in the last couple of years, as demonstrated by the election of Rick Scott to the governorship and Marco Rubio to the U.S. Senate. The Tea Party is a big part of Florida GOP politics. Yet it seems that Florida voters there understand that old Reagan line, "The fellow who agrees with me 80% of the time is not my enemy." Romney Inc. should be grateful for Disney World's apparent deliberation on this matter, as this is the time to put Gingrich away once and for all. A Newt win in Florida would damage the Romney brand beyond recognition. While Mitt faces friendlier turf in the upcoming primaries and caucus events in Nevada, Michigan, and Arizona, the whole thing will be an uphill slog if Newt pulls off another win. In my opinion, Romney doesn't need double digits, just a comfortable victory from a key swing state.

Romney Inc. has run a better, sharper, and more focused campaign in Florida. Even as the former Massachusetts Governor's tax returns have caused an earthquake of envy and anti-capitalism from Democrats and the Occupy Wall Street loons, Mitt seems to be all offense. He is hitting Newt hard on the stump, in debates, and in a series of very effective TV and web ads. The strategy in Florida has been to continue to create doubts about Newt. He has almost no chance of beating Obama, and he would have a catastrophic effect on the GOP in upcoming House, Senate, and gubernatorial races across the country. Not only would Newt's nuclear-winter effect hurt Republicans seeking federal and high-profile state offices, I believe it would negatively impact all Republican candidates. Note to party activists: if you or someone you know is running for dogcatcher in your town and you have an R after your name, you might want to wait until 2014 to consider public service if Newt Gingrich should somehow become the party's nominee! In other words if you're down ticket from Newt...you're toast!

Romney is running a better campaign in Florida, and the party is beginning to realize that flirting with candidate Gingrich might give them a bit of a rush, but as for the matrimonial commitment of nominating him... well, we all know Newt's track record when it comes to marriage. Newt's problem in this primary and in a potential general election is his own personal instability. This is the guy who wondered in his book why *Jurassic Park* shouldn't be a real project. At one point he seemed to be pushing for a legal path to statehood for future moon colonies. Mitt's latest ads are taking full advantage of the concept of Newt as the unstable and possibly fully unhinged candidate.

I believe the thing that has helped Mitt Romney most in Florida is the fact that President Obama had what seemed like three hours on national television to deliver his "Mis-State of the Union" address on Tuesday evening. Those of us who forced ourselves to watch it were subjugated to soaring rhetoric and a bloviated, revisionist view of the actual state of our union. The President has not only lost credibility for his failed policies and broken promises; he seems to have lost touch with reality as well. It's unfathomable that he dared to insist that "America's back!" and "the state of our union is getting stronger" while he casts aside economic recovery projects like the Keystone Pipeline and reforms like Simpson-Bowles. Not only that, we face complete and total uncertainty from enemies who wish us harm, like those on the Korean Peninsula and that wacky Middle Eastern madman "Achmed the Terrible!" Apparently the only person on the planet less in touch with reality than Gingrich is Obama! The President has done for Mitt Romney what no Republican challenger could have: reminded Americans that we don't want four more years of the community organizer in chief's lack of understanding of our economy, our international challenges, and the grave place many Americans find themselves today. More than 60% of our citizenry believe America is on the wrong track.

This is Florida's chance to become famous for something more than theme parks, palm trees, and senior citizens who drive with blinkers on pretty much all the time. Let me respectfully suggest that voters lay a little sunshine on the future of the GOP and our nation by doing the right thing. Not all will be lost for Newt in Florida. He and Callista might at least get a chance to enjoy that *Jurassic Park*-themed ride at Universal Studios in Orlando!

## GONE FISHIN':
### *Did Anything Happen in the Race for the White House While I Was on Vacation?*

You have perhaps missed my postings for the last couple of weeks—then again, maybe not. Even I require a vacation every now and then, and that's where I've been, all the while keeping an eye on politics and saving up for my first post-vacation column.

When last I posted, Romney Inc. was listing badly from a Newt trouncing in South Carolina. Then came Florida, where I had a chance to see first-hand how truly nasty this GOP race had become. The attack ads and the handiwork of Mitt and Newt's respective Super PACs made the beaches of the Sunshine State look a bit like Normandy! It was ugly, but at the end of the day Mitt found himself with a big win in a critical swing state. It seemed that once again Romney Inc. had found its footing. Finally, thanks to a plurality of delegates, plenty of cash, and strong debate performances, Mitt Romney was getting some legitimate respect. Ditto Nevada, where he was expected to win based largely on a big Mormon population and strong organization.

Then came the February contests in Colorado, Minnesota, and Missouri. Things went south. Again. Losing the caucus state of Missouri to Rick Santorum, where no delegates were at stake, was disappointing but not unexpected. Losing in Minnesota, where former Governor Tim Pawlenty might have been of some help, was a surprise. As the results from Colorado trickled in, it was shocking to see Romney Inc. give up all three contests to Santorum. Remember, Mitt won both Colorado and Minnesota in 2008 with 60% and 41% of the vote respectively.

The questions began anew. What's wrong with Romney? Why can't he close the deal? Is he conservative enough for Tea Party conservatives? Santorum's answer was no, and Team Santo used the surprise trifecta to raise some quick cash and breathe life in to what should by now be a long-dead campaign. Rick Santorum will not be the nominee of the party, but he's still out there. He's taken advantage of Obama's social foibles; for example, his insistence that Catholic institutions, including hospitals and schools, must provide contraceptive and abortion services as part of their healthcare plans. According to Obama, not all employees of these organizations are of Roman Catholic faith. Therefore, under Obama-Care, Catholic teachings and Catholic healthcare directives would be not allowed. Someone must have shared the concept of the separation of church and state with the POTUS, because the White House has since attempted a pivot on the issue. Their about-face still doesn't pass muster with U.S. Catholic bishops. The whole brouhaha happened leading up to the February contests, giving Santorum plenty to crow about to help him with social and religious conservatives. The base was reminded that only a guy like Rick Santorum could offer real conservatism.

Then came Saturday and yet another pair of surprises: Mitt won the CPAC straw poll in Washington (albeit narrowly) over Santorum. He followed this win by taking the Maine Caucus, which many expected Ron Paul to win. In a single day Romney bested both Santorum and the more and more insignificant Newt Gingrich among the most conservative group of GOP voters at CPAC and the libertarian-minded downeasters of Maine. Mitt was back. This guy's been counted out again and again, only to come back to life as the party's perennial frontrunner.

All eyes now move to Michigan and Arizona on February 28. Romney will do well as the favorite son in Michigan, where his father was once Governor, and in Arizona, where his immigration policy will play well among GOP voters. Fifty-nine delegates are up for grabs between the two states, which are the last significant contests until the March 5th Super Tuesday vote, where Gingrich is praying for a miracle. Romney's got the money and the delegates, and he's proven that he can win five of the nine contests held so far. The CPAC performance doesn't hurt, and he heads into Romney country in the next couple of weeks. So what can we say about Santorum, Paul, and Gingrich?

The answer: not much! Santo will hang around awhile, but is likely out after Super Tuesday. Santorum has four wins if you count Iowa, which makes him second in delegates so far. Ron Paul, whom I have skewered in my writings as everyone's crazy uncle, has all but admitted even he can't see himself as President. He doesn't believe he can win, and he's running only to make a point or two about the constitution and American liberties. Paul will stay in till the bitter end. He has plenty of money, and his supporters run on illegal substances that keep them all feeling optimistic no matter what happens. Good thing, since Paul has yet to win a single contest.

Then there's Newt: grumpy, arrogant, bitter, and quickly becoming irrelevant as we head to the home stretch. Newt needs to get out of this race before his worst instincts completely take over and he announces that he is the victim of a conspiracy of elites trained by communists to stop his presidential aspirations. Memo to Newt: Call Fox and start renegotiating your contract with Roger Ailes.

As I write this, Mitt has headed to California for a few days of rest. My sense is, however, that he won't really rest until after Super Tuesday, when the real race for the White House begins!

# BOSTON, WE HAVE A PROBLEM:
## *Mitt's Problems on His Home Turf Proving Tricky*

I opined earlier in the week that Romney Inc.'s surprise win in the CPAC straw poll, combined with a nice little win in Maine, was likely to quickly assure the narrative that he remains the GOP frontrunner. How quickly things change!

In recent days, national polls have indicated Mitt is in the fight of his life against the guy who now appears to offer a legitimate conservative alternative to the establishment: Rick Santorum. Yes, I wrote as recently as last week that Santorum could not and would not be the GOP nominee. Not so fast! Santorum, with the help of his strong social conservative credentials; surprise wins in Missouri, Colorado, and Minnesota (and the help of his millionaire sponsor, mutual fund king Foster Fries); appears poised to actually suddenly maybe, just maybe deny Romney a clear path to the nomination. It's almost unimaginable, but Romney Inc. is in real trouble in his home state of Michigan, which holds its primary on February 28th. Romney won there in 2008 with only 39% of the vote. It is the place he grew up and the place where his father was the popular Governor. The standard the national media will hold him to there will be very high.

If Mitt ekes out a win, the spin will make it sound like a loss. But what if Mitt actually loses? That would be a time for real pause. The "Boston, we have a problem" signal has already been sent. Romney's only choice is to run a two-pronged attack strategy against Santorum and Gingrich. The idea is to define Santorum as a big-spending, earmarking Washington insider to depress his conservative street cred. The Gingrich stuff is an annuity policy to make sure the former speaker doesn't somehow rise from the dead yet again. The charges are as follows: Santorum is a big spender who teamed up with Hillary Clinton. Newt teamed up with Nancy Pelosi. All are featured in a couple of tough new ads the Boston smart guys are running in Michigan, Arizona, and selected other states including Ohio, where a recent Quinnipiac poll puts Santorum ahead.

The problem for Romney is that voters are starting to catch on to his M.O. for remainin what the media and his opponents label a "weak frontrunner": using his money advantage to carpet-bomb fellow Republicans into near oblivion in order to make your own challenges seem minimal. This was the strategy used against Gingrich to great effect in Florida, and now Santorum is in the line of fire. Santorum, with his newfound momentum and the aforementioned largesse of Mr. Friess, is hitting back hard with one of the best ads of the campaign. It's a new twist on the classic mud-throwing accusation that has been around for years. This spot, titled "Rombo," has a Mitt look-a-like armed with a mud- firing submachine gun and chasing a cardboard cutout of Santorum through an abandoned warehouse. Mud splatters everywhere as the voiceover talks about the way Mitt is prone to trying to hide his own liberal record by attacking his more conservative opponents. This is a funny and engaging spot that cuts through the clutter and makes Mitt's Mr. Clean image suspect, suggesting quite literally that Romney's attempts to sling mud at his opponents will backfire. It's the best spot of the race so far, and it effectively boxes Romney into a very tough place.

With Michigan and Arizona clearly in sight and Super Tuesday looming, it has become do or die for Romney. If he loses Michigan, the whispers will turn to shouts. The money guys will start to bail. This is especially problematic for Romney given the huge campaign infrastructure and overhead they have built, which must be sustained with more and more cash each and every day. The other problem is that it costs a lot of money to wage attacks against two opponents at once in what is now becoming a national campaign. Anybody check the balance in the Romney checking account lately? By all estimates he still has the money advantage, but the burn rate on the campaign's cash is too costly, and a loss in Michigan could be the straw that breaks the camel's back. Mitt might lose in the place he was nearly guaranteed to win. He would lose momentum, as well as the stature of being the perceived frontrunner. If so, he could lose the nomination.

One final thought: Rick Santorum is a lot tougher to knock down than Newt Gingrich. Newt comes pre-packaged with the potential for ad makers to create a mini-series of attack scenarios. All of them have worked. But there is now something organic about Santorum. A fresh face? A younger, more relevant conservative that speaks to the potential longevity of the conservative cause? Bottom line: Santorum has clawed his way from nowhere to somewhere again and again. First in Iowa; then in Missouri, Colorado, and Minnesota; and now maybe in Michigan and Arizona. Santorum still has much to prove—but today in Boston, Romney Inc. knows they have a potential problem.

# TIME FOR MR. FIX-IT TO FIX IT:
### *It's Time to Change It Up Big Time!*

Dear Governor Romney:

You probably don't remember me. I had a chance to work for you for a short period of time prior to your 2008 presidential campaign. I did some early spadework in New Hampshire with you and your team. I have great respect for you personally. I believe that not only can you win the GOP nomination and the presidency, but also that you would make a damn fine President. America would be lucky to have you especially at this critical time.

That said, I would like to offer you some free advice. (I understand that free advice is worth what you pay for it, but consider this a nominal campaign contribution from me to you.) I know you have a large, talented staff, with lots of consultants, pollsters, and campaign pros—all of whom are much smarter than I am. But please bear with me at least as I offer my take.

This nomination fight should be over by now. Rick Santorum is a guy who couldn't attract a crowd at in a car wreck until a few weeks ago. But many of the most conservative in our party align themselves with the aptly named Tea Party because they are a rebellious lot who have had it with the status quo.

These folks are especially weary of you, sir. They believe you are a "conservative of convenience." They've seen the old tapes of you debating Ted Kennedy during your Senate race. You remember, the ones where you were not quite so strongly opposed to abortion and gay rights. Then there was that "Romney-Care" thing when you were Governor. The Dems jumped right on that, with the President himself giving you the left-handed compliment of serving the Massachusetts law up as a model for the President's own national healthcare reform bill. Ouch!

You have argued that the healthcare mandate in the Commonwealth was a state's rights issue and that it worked for your state. You also say you would repeal and replace Obama-Care on your first day in office. But many in the conservative base simply don't believe you. They believe your evolution to conservatism is a blatant attempt at re-packaging and they're just not buying it. You are supposed to be the frontrunner, and you were supposed to have this wrapped up by now. But the voters decide it, not you or your endorsers or all that Super PAC cash. As long as they have a totem like Rick Santorum to taunt you with, they will continue to do it.

The Boston bean counters are not helping things with their arguments, spreadsheets, and mathematical equations on the inevitability of you becoming the party's nominee. "It's done, it's over. There's no way Santorum can win a plurality of delegates in time. It's preordained... Whether or not the voters and the media like you, you are the unpleasant medicine that they will have to swallow and that's that." This is just making the anti-establishment social conservatives stay up all night trying to figure out ways to make this nomination harder, not easier, for you. Please, sir, tell your staff to stop doing this yesterday!

Instead, why not be who you are? You are a successful CEO who turned around companies and created free market economic opportunities and real private sector jobs. You turned around the Olympic Games after 9/11 at a time when our country desperately needed to feel proud. You were a damn good governor of a state that was controlled by a liberal legislature, and you still managed to stand up for the things you believed in: cutting taxes, balancing the budget, creating jobs, reducing debt, and even occasionally getting support from some of those very same Democrats. You are a fixer and a turnaround expert. So now it's time to eat a little of your own cooking and turn around your own campaign.

Here's what I suggest:

1.  Be who you are. Nothing wrong with campaign casual. After all, you don't want to come off like Richard Nixon, a guy who allegedly slept in a suit and tie. At the same time, whoever is buying you the Dad jeans from The Gap needs to be told to stop. There is a joke out there that if you do become President your Secret Service code name will be "Denim." You are a lot of things, but a jean-wearin' sheep-arder or cool college hipster you are not. Wear slacks and a blazer, and occasionally put on the presidential costume (that's a suit and tie). The jeans have become a comic metaphor for the repackaged candidate the right-of-center crowd in your own party does not like.

2.  Get a message. There is no narrative left to the story of Mitt Rom-ney's campaign. Sure, Newt hit you hard on Bain. So what? Newt has proven himself to be an intellectual nitwit only truly prepared to organize a democracy on Pluto. He got slapped hard for attacking a core tenet of the GOP: free market capitalism, for which you are the poster child. Don't be timid, get that back. Also, keep pushing the idea that Santorum and Newt have spent their whole lives in Washington, and Obama behaves like he has. Remind voters what is at stake in this election. There will be no do-over. We won't get another chance. If Barack Obama is re-elected, the effect on this country will be lasting and irreversible. Mitt, you're the guy fight-ing this for all Republicans and Independents. Tell them that! The message in this race is still jobs and the economy. If it becomes about the Republican nominee (which Obama and his billions will try to make certain) than we lose. If the race is about $4 or $5 a-gallon gasoline, over 8% unemployment, high taxes, govern-ment spending, bailouts, raising taxes and gutting our military in the most uncertain time in America since the Cold War, it becomes about him. In that case, you win. Your message should be that you are the one guy uniquely qualified to challenge the President on the very things he disdains: free markets, economic opportunity, a thriving private sector, and a government that is not growing, but shrinking. You've done it, you know how, you'll do it again. Have you seen Obama's new slogan, "America's back"? What the hell does that mean? Where does he think we went? If America was somehow

gone for a while, did it happen on his watch? How dare this ne'er-do-well, anti-capitalist, neo-socialist make such a statement about our country? America's not back, America's never left ! We've never given up, despite Barack Obama's dim-witted attempts to destroy the very soul of this country. This guy's a megalomaniac and a fraud. That's a bad combination and one you can surely beat. So talk about big ideas, reform, and America's place in the world. Give some solid policy speeches. Don't waste election-night victories thanking every two-bit political hack who jumped on the establishment bandwagon by endorsing you! You gave a victory speech in New Hampshire that was substantive and impressive. Beg Peggy Noonan to help. I know she's out of politics and writing thoughtful things for the *New York Times*, but she's the kind of storyteller who can help craft speeches that will capture the true essence of Mitt Romney. I know you like trees, and cars, and lake. (as you bizzarly stated in Michigan), so do I. But what in God's name does that have to do with you and your qualifications to turn this nation around? Project a sense of confidence and leadership like the good CEO you are.

3. It's time for them to go! Time for a retooling, rebranding, facelift, makeover, fresh start, or whatever you want to call it. Whoever is whispering in your ear (besides Ann) will need to be replaced. I'm talking about the guys who are failing to create a cohesive narrative for you. The guys whose idea it's been to promote process over vision and ideas. Do what you did at Bain. Restructure. Get the dead wood out and bring in some clever, talented people who understand you and your story verses the President's. Bottom line: this is not about the ad war. This is about articulating who you are and what you are every day in a disciplined, coherent, and effective manner. The current guys on the payroll just ain't cuttin' it. If you do in fact like to "fire people", you might want to start at Boston headquarters.

4. Target fiscal conservatives, mainstream Republicans, and those who believe you are the best candidate to beat Obama in the general. Be conservative, but don't pander to the right. It's disingenuous and they are on to you. You missed a chance to clobber that nitwit Rush Limbaugh over his ridiculous remarks about a young woman who

happened to have a different view of reproductive rights than he did. Fine to disagree, but you had a chance to be the adult in the room and tell Limbaugh that he was a bloated gasbag who stepped over the line. You should have told him that a real man and a true conservative does not call young women crude, juvenile, locker-room names. Instead, you dodged, and in the process missed a chance to show them who you are and what you're made of. The endorsement thing? It's not working so well either. You have more endorsement deals than Tiger Woods did before his domestic problems. Enough already! All these pols piling on are only adding to the right's perception of your establishment problem. Tell them to stop rolling out establishment types. It's bad box office!

5. Start running stuff about what you will do differently. Shoot a great policy speech in front of a throng of enthusiastic voters and kids who can't get jobs because of Obama's economic policies, and cut it into a powerful TV campaign and web video series. Talk about tomorrow, not yesterday. As for Santorum: time for Pat Toomey to go on the air in Pennsylvania.

6. Use Ann more! She's good and crowds love her!

7. Let your sons introduce you more often. The family thing seems to be working for Santorum. Even Newt uses those professorial daughters of his.

8. Slow it down a tad. When you're speaking at a town hall event, don't act like you are trying desperately to force every person in the hall to like you. It's like a comedian begging for laughs. If you stick to your big ideas, core message points, and the fundamentals of this race, you will win them over just by being you.

9. Tell them your view of the world. As you know better than anyone, in a global economy one needs to understand global economics. You do. Our energy policy is critical. The imbalance of our trade agreements with other countries creates a lack of economic opportunities. Finally, with madmen running Syria, Iran, and North Korea, and some new uncertainty in our relations with China and the

former Soviet Union, we need a President who understands that we must maintain a clear awareness of our friends and enemies abroad. Obama can't do it, Santorum won't do it, and God knows we don't want Newt to try doing it!!

10. Relax! I know that's easy for me to say. But you're quite qualified on any number of levels to be President. Try to lose the nervous laugh. You don't have to answer every question within nanoseconds. Remember that gaffes (which we are all capable of) usually happen when you are tired, overscheduled, or off message. Take a breath.

At the end of the day, the social conservatives will come your way. The one thing they distrust far more than you is Barack Obama. Give them a chance to come to you on their terms. In the process, please don't lose your street cred with the rest of the voters you will need in the general election. Rick Santorum has a ceiling, and he's just about there. He too will come around. The convention in Tampa is still a long way off. You have time for America to see you bring this thing together masterfully. All this talk by the lefties in the mainstream media about a brokered convention? You and I both know your campaign and the RNC will employ bigger, badder whips than any defensive line any NFL team could put up. Speeches will be made and deals will be cut. At the end of the day Republicans will rally around the one guy who they believe can and will defeat Barack Obama in November. That person is you! There will simply never be a brokered convention. Ignore that jive! Like I said, free advice is only worth what you pay for it, but keep your chin up and carry on. This nomination is yours and the Oval office is in need of new curtains!

★

# CHAPTER FORTY-FOUR

# HEY SANTO, YOU'RE TOAST:
### *Santorum's Silly Holdout Turns Into Bad Box Office and a Worse Career Move!*

"If I win Illinois, I win the nomination!" So said Senator Rick Santorum last week, after bumbling his way through a disastrous week of campaigning. This included a stop in Puerto Rico, where he further pushed aside potential Latino voters by insisting that English must be adopted as the territory's official language as a pre-condition to statehood.

Santo then went on to make the case that he was the only candidate who could win in the important Midwest, although it seems he apparently doesn't consider Michigan or Ohio the Midwest. He attempted a pivot on this one by correcting himself with another statement suggesting he meant the heartland, which must not include Illinois either!

Santorum lost Illinois even before the voting began on Tuesday. He didn't even qualify for about ten delegates, as he failed to get himself on the ballot in the state's important 13th Congressional District. The Senator and his campaign are somehow still not ready for primetime. Tuesday night, however, was the kicker. Santo returned home to Pennsylvania to deliver his victory speech (after getting crushed in Illinois by Romney, 47% to 35%). The Senator took great pride in giving a rambling stem-winder, in which he regularly and without any apparent preparation tried to make lemons out of lemonade. He insisted that next week's contest in Louisiana would be big for hi—and so will Wisconsin and Pennsylvania, where he intends to "win a lot of delegates." Let's give Santo Louisiana, unless of course Buddy Roemer mounts a strong last-minute write-in campaign. It's a very conservative place, and his kind of crowd. I might even concede Wisconsin to Santorum, as it too is a socially conservative state with a very strong right-to-life movement. Pennsylvania? Not so fast! Yes, it's Santorum's home state and the place they know him best. He's leading in the polling right now with about 35%. That's all this guy can garner in his home state? I smell trouble.

Romney Inc.'s impressive victory in Illinois was best demonstrated in exit polling. Polls showed him winning overwhelmingly with voters who understand the only issue that really matters in this elephant parade: the ability to deny President Obama a second term. 71% of Illinois voters said they support Romney because they believe he was the candidate they thought could beat the President in November. Mitt seemed to begin to bring conservatives home, winning 43% of the conservative vote versus Santorum's 39% of voters who self-identify as very conservative. 43% percent of voters said Romney is "not conservative enough." 43% said he was "conservative enough" and that his positions in their view were "just about right." This metric also speaks to Mitt's ability to appeal to moderate and independent voters in a general election.

Why is this important? It's a long way to Tampa and a longer way until November. Does anyone think conservatives will not vote? Better yet, does anyone think that once Mitt is the Republican nominee fiscal and social conservatives will not coalesce behind him? Hold the base and attract independent voters: that's how you win a general election.

In the land of Lincoln, Romney demonstrated an ability to show that he is the establishment candidate, the conservative-enough candidate, and the candidate who can attract independent swing voters.

Back to the speeches. Santo takes to the stage in Gettysburg and apologizes that the "big crowd outside couldn't get into the hall." Memo to Santo: next time, don't hold your victory party at a Pizza Hut! My sense is they went for the small loser's venue, hoping to get a big enough crowd to make it look like somebody in Pennsylvania actually knows or cares about Santorum. The rambling speech, during which the Senator took the time to jab Mitt for having used a teleprompter in his speech, was a laugh riot. Believe me, Senator—everyone there knew that there wasn't a teleprompter within ten miles of your speech. I feel bad for the Santorum kids too. Seems like every Tuesday they gather somewhere and stand behind their dad in the dorky sweater vests, knowing they're gonna take grief about it from kids on the bus when they get to back to school.

The Santorum line that he is the only conservative choice to defeat Obama has become a silly caricature for a campaign that is well past its sell date. Santorum is no longer just hurting the party. Even if he wins in a few more states, he's now hurting himself. It's time for a reality check at Camp Santo!

The horse is headed to the barn. The nomination process for GOP challenger to President Obama is as clear as it was when all this started. Romney is now the de facto nominee. Someone just needs to get that message to Rick Santorum, who still believes he's fighting the battle of Gettysburg.

# OBAMAVILLE:

*From the People Who Brought You Rick Santorum!*

This is a serious election, perhaps the most serious presidential election in our lifetimes. How many times have you heard that one? It gets said during every election by both parties. Third-party nutcases like the nudists, the vegans, and the Ron Paul supporters also sing this familiar refrain. The fact is 2012 *is* a very serious election, and certainly most Republicans and a good number of independent voters know it.

We have a country with ballooning debt and unemployment still over 8% (using the President's numbers). The President promised us an energy policy that would decrease America's reliance on foreign oil, yet he opposes and ridiculously over-regulates offshore drilling and ANWAR. He has recently even rejected the Keystone Pipeline project.

He is in way over his head on foreign affairs. He has some serious challenges in both understanding and articulating his vision for America's place in an increasingly dangerous and unpredictable world. In other words, this guy is by almost any reasonable measure an abject failure.

That's the one reason that this election is so important. Republicans need a serious and capable candidate to provide contrast, and a very different prescription for the problems that face us in the years to come.

Last week, Rick Santorum's campaign released a web video ad cleverly entitled "Obamaville." The spot is a combination of a horror movie trailer and sci-fi fantasy that tries to get us to consider what another term of Obama might bring. The spot is well-produced and well-edited, with some truly disturbing images. It looks like it was put together by the Hollywood love child of David Lynch and Quentin Tarantino! This thing makes the *Hunger Games* trailer look like a theme party promotion for a nine-year-olds. It's so over-the-top that it actually becomes silly. Maybe it's the music track from *Dark Shadows* or the fact that the male voice-over sounds like Vincent Price on steroids. This thing is highly entertaining and will go down in the annals of campaign comedy as the funniest, most sophomoric attempt at humor since Stephen Colbert formed his Super PAC. The problem is that Santo and company are serious. This is, after all, a serious election. There are serious issues at hand.

Why trivialize the very essence of the Republican message against the President? Most voters will watch this attempt to portray Armageddon in a second Obama term as an *SNL* short. This whole idea is the wrong tone and makes the entire case against Obama look ridiculous.

I hope the guys at Santo Central all had a good laugh over this one, because it's exactly the kind of spot that makes it to air when the kids are left alone in the editing room without adult supervision.

Santorum is as in over his head as Obama. It's time he headed back to the dreaded private sector, where he and his ad goons can maybe get a development deal with the Sci-Fi Channel. Serious elections, serious issues, and serious candidates would never allow this stupid drivel to be produced. Paging the babysitter!

# CHAPTER FORTY-SIX

# WHERE'S NEWT:

## *Alone, Rudderless, and Incoherent in the Political Wilderness*

Has anybody seen Newt Gingrich lately? Since not winning a delegate or a primary or a caucus contest after his home state of Georgia, the anemic former Speaker appears to have gone underground. Maybe Newt's getting ready to announce that he's teaming up with Nancy Pelosi again to get the old love seat out of mothballs. Maybe Newt and Callista are working on a new film, an epic biography of Saul Alinsky? Now that would be a real screen gem!

Sure, I see Newt around now and again. Usually he's on some cable gab-fest talking about nothing particularly interesting or compelling. The trouble with this image is that it is so un-Newt! Gingrich is smart and interesting, but of late he's acting more like a bitter, misdirected malcontent nomadically roaming the country like a crazed big-idea circus act without the big top.

It's sad, really. Speaker Gingrich is a serious person with some pretty grandiose ideas. He might not be presidential material, as the GOP appears to have figured out, but he's always managed to make himself interestin-—until recently. Newt needs to stop the bus, end the campaign, and get back to his job on Fox News. He can keep giving speeches, writing books, and teaching his new college course: "Newtonian Political Science on a Newly Colonized Mars."

I like the Speaker. I have had the pleasure of meeting with him and talking with him. I even moderated a 90-minute debate with he and Jon Huntsman during the campaign. He is above this senseless journey he is currently on. Newt, you're hurting the brand and the GOP. Please go home and begin working on a really interesting and thoughtful convention speech. It is time for all good men (and women) to come to the aid of their country. We're waiting...

## HOTEL FEBREZE HAS GONE TO SANTORUM'S HEAD:
### *The Senator Is Apparently Suffering from Holiday Inn Brain!*

It's known in traveler's circles as Holiday Inn Brain. It's a serious condition that affects business travelers, political candidates, and road warriors of every stripe after they've been overexposed to the lumpy beds, worn carpets, slimy shower curtains, the distinct smell of Fabreeze, and stale bagel and runny egg buffet breakfasts of budget hotels. It goes by other names: Red Roof Brain, Courtyard by Marriott Fatigue, Comfort Inn Confusional Syndrome, and the dreaded Best Western Dementia. Symptoms of having been on the road for too often manifest themselves as follows: saying or doing stupid things with increasing regularity, stepping in it more often than usual, making ridiculous comments and then losing your temper with the traveling press when they question you. Victims can even manifest symptoms by abandoning all rational principles and actually suggesting that Barack Obama would be best left in place as leader of the free world. Somebody call 911!

It's a serious and debilitating affliction, and it's pretty clear Senator Rick Santorum has a bad case of it. In recent weeks the Senator has said some really dumb things as he desperately struggles on against the sad realities of delegate math in his quixotic quest for the presidency. I understand his frustration. He's the conservative, damn it! He's the genuine article! Mitt Romney is the mad scientist who first breathed life into the healthcare reform initiative in Massachusetts, which led to that horrific monster known as Obama-Care! Rick is different. He is the real deal. Not fake, not phony, not disingenuous, and not pandering. He is the blue-collar guy who came from nowhere. Why don't they get it? Why don't more voters see it? How does Romney Inc. keep coming back to fight another day? It's due to a lot of things, but the recent Santorum gaffes haven't helped.

A few weeks ago, Santo went to the tiny Caribbean island known as Puerto Rico (which, by the way, is a U.S. territory) and told the good voters there that until they adopted English as their primary language, they should not be granted statehood. As you can imagine, this didn't go over big with the locals.

Then the Senator made the remark that President Obama would be a better choice than Romney in a general election. Huh? Then he said that no matter what the unemployment rate might be, it would have no bearing on the things he wanted to talk about in the campaign. He included a lot of social issues like abortion, gay rights, contraception, and other ditties that always lose elections for Republicans. On Sunday, Santo showed how advanced his Holiday Inn Brain problem had advanced when he suggested that Mitt was "the worst possible Republican candidate" to face President Obama in a general election. This thing has become serious, and it's time for immediate treatment.

The sooner Senator Santorum takes a hard look at this thing, the sooner he can be removed from those cheap hostelries responsible for his current condition. The prescription: end the campaign. Be classy, endorse Mitt Romney, and get home to your own bed in Virginia. You'll feel better in no time, and so will the rest of the GOP. And just think of all those Holiday Inn points he will have earned to be used another time—perhaps on another campaign where you might just be considered the establishment candidate.

## MITT-A-SKETCH:
### *The Steve Jobs of Jobs?*

In 1917, with the merger of several small toy companies in Byron, Illinois, a family business was born. The Ohio Art Company manufactured novelties, packaging tins, and children's toys. The family business chugged along for years, until it unveiled what would become its breakthrough product in 1959: the Etch-A-Sketch. (I assumed the Etch-A-Sketch was invented sometime during the Truman administration, but alas it and I share the same birth year!)

The bright red toy in its clunky case was a must-have in every home. Kids learned hand-eye coordination and explored their artistic side by turning two large white knobs to manipulate a hidden internal stylus that would create images on the screen. If you made a mistake or didn't like what you created, you could just turn the thing over, shake it a few times, and any mark you made disappeared! You started again fresh with a clean slate. The toy remained a top-seller, pushing out over 150,000 units after its inception. Pretty impressive for something that could be used without batteries or electricity.

Sadly, America moved on. In recent decades, the technology boom has allowed kids to own toys and electronics that stimulate all the senses and allow one to click one's way to art, literature, and Facebook. As America went high-tech, the tech-less toy category began to lose steam. So went the fortunes of the Etch-A-Sketch. Falling sales forced Ohio Art to send the product to China to be manufactured at a fraction of the cost of American production.

The Etch-a-Sketch was re-discovered and brought back to relevance by Romney Inc. in the midst of the 2012 GOP presidential campaign. When it comes to turning around American companies, Mitt and his team haven't lost their touch.

It all started when Romney Inc. senior advisor Eric Fehrnstrom appeared on a cable TV gabfest to provide some perspective on why Mitt hasn't been damaged by the protracted GOP primary battle. Fehrnstrom reasoned that in the 2012 general election campaign, when the choice becomes Romney or Obama, American voters will collectively hit the reset button. Then he used a metaphor that brought one of America's most iconic products roaring back to relevance: "It's almost like an Etch-A-Sketch. You can kind of shake it up and start all over again."

Suddenly, the Etch-A-Sketch became the hottest toy in America once again. Romney's rivals, Rick Santorum and Newt Gingrich, dispatched their staffs to buy up as many of the toys as possible. They held the clunky red tablet up for all to see as a symbol of the candidate who stood for nothing and whose campaign believed he could just erase all the bad memories, gaffes, charges, countercharges, alleged flip-flops and interparty strife of the campaign. The metaphor may have invited the pokes, but the effect was incredible.

Etch-A-Sketch began trending on Twitter. The news media, the blogosphere, and talking heads went crazy. Everywhere you looked there was an Etch-A-Sketch debate, and Romney was right in the middle of it. So was Ohio Art.

Moments after Fehrnstrom's comment, the phones began ringing at the company's Illinois offices. Demand for the product soared. The company's stock, which had closed at just under $4 a share the day before, would finish at $12.50 a share (a 52-week high!) Etch-A-Sketch had gone from near-irrelevance to suddenly being low-tech cool. It was now known as the EAS. In the next few days, it would become Amazon's fastest-selling product, jumping 1,200 spots in rank and landing as the 110th most popular toy item. The boys at Romney Inc. have been saying Mitt was a turnaround expert: first at Bain, then the Olympics, then Massachusetts, and now Etch-A-Sketch!

Nicole Gresh, a spokeswoman for Ohio Art, said, "We feel our stock has gone up over the last 24 hours due to an increase in exposure and an increase in anticipated product sales. While it is too early to tell what type of spike the product will achieve, we are confident we will see a spike in Etch-a-Sketch sales." Talk about turning around the economy!

"This is the first time we've seen EAS go viral so quickly," said Martin Killgallon, Sr., Vice President of Marketing and Production for Ohio Art. Mr. Killgallon, I'm betting this is the *only* time you've seen the EAS go viral.

This past week, my friend Alex Castellanos wrote a very smart piece for *Politico* in which he asks an interesting question. What if Fehrnstrom was right? What if, in fact, the American people will hit the reset button after Romney officially becomes the nominee? They very well might. The economy is a mess, gas prices are headed still headed higher, unemployment is still over 8%, and 76% of Americans believe the country is on "the wrong track."

Maybe Fehrnstrom knew exactly what he was saying. Maybe the American people will quickly forget the Republican family squabble of the past year and move on, looking for a stark contrast to the mess Obama has created. My bet is, they will. That makes Mitt Romney a viable alternative and a relevant choice for Republicans and independent almost as relevant as the new and improved EAS.

Romney the turnaround guy is the right antidote for the maladies made nearly unbearable by the Obama regime. Mitt and his team have managed to slog through a tough race. They've lived to amass a plurality of delegates and a strong narrative as to why he is the most electable candidate of the lot to face the President in a general election. In the process, Romney Inc. has helped show us how you turn American ingenuity and a little promotion into real private-sector success. Just ask Ohio Art!

If you're wondering what the hot toy will be in the coming year, keep an eye on the Etch-A-Sketch. I understand Romney Inc. has some brand extensions in mind that could create an even bigger boom for the company. These include the Etch-An-Air, The Etch-A-Pod, Etch-Tunes and the Etch-Pad. These will still be red, but I'm told they will be a tad sleeker and cooler-looking. You might want to order one now, because the lines at the EAS stores will be long and cold when we get toward the holiday season. Nice work, Mr. Fehrnstrom!

# ANN ROMNEY NEVER WORKED
# A DAY IN HER LIFE:
### *When Wild Liberal Moonbeams Attack*

The Obama White House and its official and unofficial surrogates have been insulting female voters for months now. They're suggesting that Romney and the GOP have a critical gender problem. Please!

I know a lot of smart women—not all of them Republicans—who are professionals, working women, or moms who work in the home. While they are concerned about many issues, they are independent enough and smart enough to triage their concerns in this election.

Of course women are concerned about their reproductive health rights. They're also concerned about their kids, education, the environment, and the economy! To suggest that they are not capable of sorting through the issues of the day and triaging them in perspective is more than a little insulting. It's a blatant attempt to pander to women voters, and that's a dangerous path for the Obamanistas!

Last night on CNN some left-wing moonbeam not officially speaking for the Obama campaign attempted to push the gender gap foolishness to the point of near hysterics. She suggested that "Ann Romney has never worked a day in her life." Wow! I haven't heard gender-biased rhetoric like that since Hillary made it clear she was not prepared to stay home and bake cookies like the rest of the gals!

The White House attempted to push itself away from the leftist moonbeam's rant, but the damage was done. Romney Inc. didn't take long to jump on the gaffe, using its own secret weapon: Mrs. Romney herself. To suggest that a woman isn't working who has served on countless boards, performed community service, and been a public servant and a political activist in her own right, all while raising five sons, is an assault on every woman in America. Obama's arrogance will come back to haunt him. Women who work in the home raising their kids? Evil! Rich people? Evil! People who believe differently than the Obama lefties? Evil!

The personal attack on Ann Romney by some Democrat hack is unfortunate, but it is a clear example of how far this President and his supporters will go to win as ugly as possible in November. There's only one problem. Female voters are onto the President and they are smart enough and independent enough to speak for themselves at the ballot box. That will be enough to send this President packing, along with his supporters who wish to divide our country based on gender, race, or class.

## GAME, SET, MITT!
*Now the Real Fun Begins*

Yesterday in Connecticut, Mitt Romney began the general election campaign and the all-important run-up to the GOP convention. With Rick Santorum bowing out following the Easter weekend, the path is now clear for Romney Inc. to steam towards the nomination. There are still two other guys ostensibly in the race. The problem is they are less relevant in GOP political circles right now than Tom Dewey. In another week both Ron Paul and Newt Gingrich could wind up as Jeopardy questions.

Q: "They were the two remaining hold-out GOP candidates running for President after early April 2012."

A: "Who were Newt Gingrich and Ron Paul?"

Santorum has made the right choice, and none too soon. He has indicated that he will work to bring the party together and defeat President Obama. He's done it with class. He has the right to be proud of a race that ran for months leading up to Iowa, where he sat at 1% in the polls. In some of the early GOP cable debates, Santorum's podium position was so far out of camera range that they might as well have placed him in the alley. But he fought his way through and bowed out with grace. I suspect we will see him again down the road, perhaps in another quest for the White House. Well done, Senator.

As for the general election, the Obamanistas have wasted no time in attempting to change the subject from jobs and the economy to class warfare. The President went to Boca Raton and Palm Beach this week to remind people that it's in vogue to hate rich people. The successful, the entrepreneurs, the small business owners, those who have risked capital and succeeded: they must be punished. What's even stranger is that after Obama's eat the rich rant, he promptly headed to a couple of fundraising events raising millions of dollars from the very fat cats and corporate jet owners he so despises. Perhaps these wealthy Obama elitists view these fund raisers as part of paying their "fair share!"

This race is about jobs, the economy, the deficit, and the debt. These are the very things President Obama does not want to discuss, because his policies have clearly failed the American people, halted any semblance of an economic recovery, and have led many Americans to simply give up. Obama wants to talk about the Buffett rule (I'm pretty sure he means Warren, not Jimmy). This is his attempt to set up successful business owners and entrepreneurs as the bad guys responsible for everything wrong with the country. He claims they don't pay their fair share in taxes. Has anyone informed the President that nearly 80% of the taxes collected in this country paid are by the wealthiest Americans? Has anyone at the CBO or the IRS bothered to remind him that even if he were to tax the rich more, estimates are that the revenues collected would account for about $80 billion? Now that's nothing to sneeze at, but here's an interesting fact: if the government were to collect that much every year (assuming the evil rich don't hire good lawyers and tax advisors to find legal loopholes around the heist) it would take 250 years to collect in taxes what Barack Obama has spent in the last year alone. $80 billion? That's exactly enough to run the Obama government for a grand total of...8 days!

Strengthening our economy, creating real jobs, and giving all Americans a chance to dream big and be successful is the foundation of our market-driven economy. This is the stuff all voters care most about this election. Republicans and independent voters in key swing states will decide this election. That's right in Mitt Romney's wheelhouse, and that's what has the Robin Hood crowd at the White House so worried.

This election will be hard-fought and close. Most people in America don't hate the rich. They aspire to have a chance at real economic success themselves. Most people realize that the people who sign their paychecks are the ones who employ them, provide their healthcare, and give them the chance to grow and succeed. That's the American dream. That's why come November, in spite of the class-warfare rhetoric coming for the White House, it will be game, set, Mitt for America.

# AFTERWORD

**On May 2, 2012, former** House Speaker Newt Gingrich stood surrounded by family and supporters in a Washington, DC hotel ballroom. The Speaker spent fifteen minutes talking about his campaign and the issues he thought were important. He spoke of his wife, his family, and his dedicated supporters. Gingrich indicated that he was formally suspending his campaign, ending a year-long odyssey in the quest for the Republican nomination. At one point in his remarks, Gingrich said, "People ask me if Mitt Romney is conservative enough. My answer: compared to Barack Obama?" Some in the press reported the Speaker's reference to Romney as tepid at best.

The Romney campaign responded by issuing a one-sentence statement: "Newt Gingrich has brought creativity and intellectual vitality to American political life."

The Speaker won just two states—South Carolina and his native Georgia—and amassed a total of 138 delegates, while raising over $23 million. He has not yet officially endorsed Mitt Romney. Maybe in Tampa?

On April 10th, in Gettysburg, Pennsylvania, Rick Santorum's campaign came to an abrupt but not unexpected end. "We made a decision over the weekend that, while this presidential race for us is over, and we will suspend our campaign effective today, we are not done fighting," Santorum said as he stood with family and supporters in front of an audience of mostly press.

Santorum had posed the strongest challenge to Romney. But as the campaign wore on and the losses piled up, the campaign finally, reluctantly saw the writing on the wall. Of even greater concern to the former Senator was the health of his daughter Bella, who was at the time of his campaign suffering complications from a rare genetic disorder.

Over the course of his campaign, Santorum spent $22.3 million, won 11 states, and collected 267 delegates. He did not endorse Mitt Romney officially until nearly a month later.

On May 14th, Ron Paul announced that he would not compete in states that have not yet voted. In other words, he was heading home to the Blue Planet. A day later a campaign spokesman would adamantly state that the Paul campaign was not over, but that it was "maximizing resources." However, choosing not to compete in the upcoming primaries meant that the campaign was effectively done.

This ended the congressman's third run for the presidency. Ron Paul raised and spent $39.7 million. He did not place first in any state, but managed to secure 137 delegates. The mother ship is still orbiting earth waiting for further instructions. As of this writing no delegates have been harmed or released.

On May 29th, Mitt Romney won the Texas primary and passed the 1,144-delegate mark needed to unofficially clinch the Republican presidential nomination. Romney raised and spent more than $120 million to win over 1,500 delegates and the nomination.

As of this writing, he has not yet contacted me to help draft his inaugural address.

www.ingramcontent.com/pod-product-compliance
Lightning Source LLC
Chambersburg PA
CBHW020852090426
42736CB00008B/344